At Your Fingertips

USING EVERYDAY DATA TO IMPROVE SCHOOLS

KAREN LEVESQUE

DENISE BRADBY

KRISTI ROSSI

PETER TEITELBAUM

MPR Associates, Inc.

National Center for Research in Vocational Education

American Association of School Administrators

SUPPORTED BY

THE OFFICE OF VOCATIONAL AND ADULT EDUCATION

U.S. DEPARTMENT OF EDUCATION

MPR Associates, Inc.

2150 Shattuck Avenue, Suite 800

Berkeley, CA 94704

800-677-6987

Fax: 510-849-0794

E-mail: services@mprinc.com

Website: http://www.mprinc.com

National Center for Research in Vocational Education

University of California at Berkeley

2030 Addison Street, Suite 500

Berkeley, CA 94720

American Association of School Administrators

1801 North Moore Street

Arlington, VA 22209

This publication was prepared pursuant to a grant (Carl D. Perkins Vocational Education Act, P.L. 98-524, Grant No. V051A30003-96A/V051A30004-96A) to the National Center for Research in Vocational Education, University of California at Berkeley, from the Office of Vocational and Adult Education, U.S. Department of Education. Points of view or opinions do not necessarily represent official U.S. Department of Education position or policy.

ISBN 0-9662883-0-0

Contributing MPR Associates Staff:

President: E. Gareth Hoachlander

Director of Curriculum and Professional Development: David R. Mandel

Production Manager: Barbara E. Kridl

Senior Editor: Andrea Livingston

Graphic Designer/Desktop Publisher: Leslie Retallick

Editorial/Production Staff: Karyn Madden, Mary Sukkestad, Francesca Tussing

Design by LekasMiller, Walnut Creek, CA

Printing and Binding by George Lithograph, Brisbane, CA

preface

Educating our children is one of the most human and most familiar activities that we as a society undertake. Yet, it remains one of our least well-understood enterprises. While much has been learned about what works in schools and what does not—that is, what exemplary practices look like and what constitutes damaging practice—many of our most accomplished teachers are often surprised about the wide range in the levels of competency among their students. With cognitive research just beginning to provide us with a window on how the young and the old learn, we do not have all the answers about how to run a first-rate school or how to help all students reach their potential.

Teaching and learning remain a mixture of art and science, of trial and error, and, when executed well, of gradually improving and perfecting one's practice as well as the curriculum and culture of the school. There are no cookbook recipes on the shelf that can be applied to assure that the result will be satisfactory in the wide variety of contexts that characterize American education today.

Given this situation, it is not surprising that educators do not usually rush to quantify the critical aspects of schooling, nor do they particularly trust those who do or the results of their efforts. This suspicion is natural, given the issues under consideration and is probably quite healthy, as education data often provide a patina of certainty that is not well deserved. However, being blind to the underlying truths that often exist in quantitative measures is shortsighted. In fact, precisely because the mysteries, charms, and beauty of education often mask what is happening and why particular results occur, be they positive or negative, quantitative analyses can be a powerful tool. If applied well, such analytical work can uncover what is occurring beneath the surface in our schools. It can alert us to unexpected triumphs and to unforeseen problems. It can tell us if new initiatives are having their desired effects, are provoking a set of unintended consequences, or both. We can learn if implementation of promising ideas is proceeding as planned or is being compromised by unexpected changes in the school district. And, as we seek to educate our children in a manner that emphasizes both excellence and equity, we can develop measures that assure we do no harm.

The development of *At Your Fingertips* was grounded in these beliefs—that well-organized quantitative knowledge about how schools operate and what students know and are able to do can be extraordinarily powerful. At a time when it is popular to distrust data, to take the position that statistics can be made to support any stance, the authors of this workbook believe that ignoring the hard reality that education statistics often present does a tremendous disservice to our children and our communities. At a time when education is widely understood to be the key to a healthy and prosperous future, those who lead our schools, who are responsible for educating the nation's youth, and the public at large, need the best tools available to gauge accurately how well schools are functioning and how well our children are learning. Consequently, *At Your Fingertips* is designed to help school people systematically marshal valid, reliable, and trustworthy data in a manner that will allow them to think clearly about how they might most effectively dedicate their knowledge, skills, and energies to the common purposes and responsibilities they share for educating the nation's youth.

At Your Fingertips does not assume that a particular pedagogical approach that is working well for a school in Chicago is going to be the best approach in Little Rock, or that organizational arrangements that appear highly effective in Tucson will translate well to those in Baltimore, although they well might. What it does assume is that professionals who work in our schools have a common interest in seeing that all students succeed, and that committed professionals working together can both devise sound instructional approaches that fit well with the traditions, history, culture, and demographics of the school; with the knowledge and skills of the student body; and with the faculty's own goals, values, talents, and beliefs; and, concurrently, design performance measurement systems that are compatible with these perspectives. *At Your Fingertips* is also built on the presumption that much of the data needed to make this happen already reside nearby in school and district offices, in teachers' own records, and in readily accessible public data banks. Not infrequently, such resources are overlooked and undervalued because they have been created to satisfy someone else's agenda. Schools regularly receive orders to produce what seem like great mounds of data, be it in the form of student tests or attendance records or budgets. However, while school people left to their own devices might not choose to devote their scarce time to such pursuits, this information, when organized well and joined with other useful data, can often be turned to the school's advantage.

At Your Fingertips seeks to do just this. We think it can achieve this result—first, by providing an orderly process for considering the various factors that can contribute to a powerful performance measurement system, and second, by sharing our knowledge about the core characteristics of a sound system and a set of promising approaches to data analysis that can "bring statistics to life" and help both educators and the general public have a richer appreciation of how well schools are satisfying their missions. The news will not always be good, but bad news is better than ignorance.

A school that is willing to examine itself critically is one that will increase the odds that its students will succeed. Such a school will also find that it has a new and effective means to communicate in a very powerful way with its parents, others in the system, and the community at large. In fact, just sharing information about how the school is functioning is such an unusual act that it will often yield a measure of good will that is invaluable to efforts to test new curricular and instructional approaches. Internally, the availability of such information can lead to a new and healthy conversation among the faculty—one that promotes reflection on practice, healthy skepticism about trendy ideas, and a school culture that values professional knowledge and expertise and finds ways to channel and use it to yield the greatest good for the greatest number.

At Your Fingertips has been created to support grass roots, bottom-up education improvement strategies that depend on the initiative, commitment, and energy of front-line professionals. It is up to the users to decide what is important, what are their school's highest priorities, and how much time can be allocated to building a meaningful system. While top-down reforms can be effective, by themselves they are unlikely to be a sufficient response to the demands for excellence and equity the nation faces today. Because well-intentioned state and national efforts to hold students to high standards need to be complemented by a host of ongoing local actions, finding ways to encourage, support, and reward home-grown local school improvement initiatives is crucial. *At Your Fingertips* can contribute to such efforts since it assists in the planning and monitoring of significant departures from the status quo. Taking calculated risks in the interest of children has typically not been encouraged in American schools, while playing it safe has been. If this publication can play a role in righting this balance, its authors will know their time has been well spent.

Today, our schools face the toughest of challenges—providing a quality education not only for an elite few but also for the entire student body. Such an education should prepare young people to participate fully in our democratic institutions and to live productive and rewarding lives in a world where science and technology play increasingly dominant roles. To meet this challenge head-on, schools cannot sit back and coast. We hope that *At Your Fingertips* will reward those educators who are committed to building better futures for the youngsters in their charge by providing them with a means to better govern their professional lives.

GARY HOACHLANDER
President
MPR Associates, Inc.

DAVID R. MANDEL
Director
MPR Center for Curriculum
and Professional Development

Berkeley, California
March 1998

Foreword

In our efforts to improve our schools, we often overlook a set of resources that are so commonplace they fail to attract our attention—the data we typically gather on students, teachers, and our local communities. If knowledge is power, there ought to be a variety of creative ways to take advantage of such resources, and *At Your Fingertips: Using Everyday Data to Improve Schools* attempts to do just this.

It is not a foolproof book of recipes. It is not a paint-by-numbers approach to innovation. Rather, it is designed to assist groups of educators who share a set of common goals advance their agenda in a systematic way. It does this by encouraging teachers, administrators, other educators, and community members to be crystal clear about what they are attempting to accomplish, how they plan to get there, and on what basis their efforts are to be judged.

At Your Fingertips encourages and supports home-grown, locally designed school improvement initiatives. It recognizes that all efforts to improve schools, no matter how well intentioned, will not always succeed and that we have an obligation to the children in our charge to do no harm and proceed carefully as we implement new policies and practices. We also have an obligation not to settle for the status quo if and when our schools are not providing an excellent education for all children.

Because it embodies these values that the American Association of School Administrators holds dear, we are pleased to join with MPR Associates and the National Center for Research in Vocational Education to bring this publication to our members and the larger elementary and secondary education community.

The data our schools regularly gather, at significant expense, can and ought to be put to good use. Well organized, the information can help us focus our attention on our most intractable problems, alert us to unexpected and unwanted developments, and let us recognize and celebrate our true, hard-won accomplishments.

PAUL D. HOUSTON
Executive Director
American Association of School Administrators

Arlington, Virginia
March 1998

Acknowledgments

The authors want to thank all those who contributed to the creation of this publication. Many people were involved in developing the model, testing the materials, and reviewing the written product. We would like especially to thank the New Castle County Vocational-Technical School District in Delaware, the Georgia Department of Children and Youth Services, the Harrisburg Steelton-Highspire Technical School in Pennsylvania, and the Ohio Department of Education for piloting the *At Your Fingertips* model and offering valuable feedback. We would also like to thank the many educators who attended *At Your Fingertips* workshops at the following summer conferences in 1995 and helped us refine the model and materials: the National Center for Research in Vocational Education (NCRVE)'s *Urban Schools Network* Summer Institute, the Southern Regional Education Board Summer Conference, and the Jobs for the Future Summer Conference.

We would like to acknowledge the careful reading of the workbook by R. Ken Clark, Superintendent of the Kelseyville School District in California; Dean Peterson, Administrator of Special Services in the Glendale Union High School District in Arizona; Erika Nielsen Andrew of NCRVE; and Gary Hoachlander, David Mandel, Paula Hudis, and Mikala Rahn of MPR Associates. Their expert knowledge and insight helped ensure that *At Your Fingertips* is practical and instructive, while also being respectful of the unique visions that schools bring to improvement efforts.

Finally, we would like to thank NCRVE and the Office of Vocational and Adult Education for their ongoing support and vision during development of this workbook.

Table of Contents

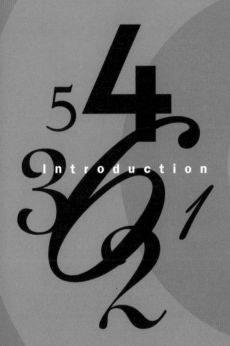

Introduction

Most schools and school districts across the nation maintain a wide variety of educational data. Examples of these data include average daily attendance rates (ADA), graduation rates, transcript data including course enrollments and grades, and standardized achievement test scores. Although these data can serve many purposes, they are typically used to satisfy administrative requirements, rather than to support improvement efforts. For instance, schools may report ADA to the state education agency, provide transcripts to postsecondary institutions, and report grades and test scores to parents. However, educators rarely examine these data to assess *in a systematic way* the quality of teaching and learning at their school.

At Your Fingertips is a workbook designed to help educators take advantage of a variety of local data to better manage, monitor, and improve schools. It is intended for teachers, administrators, and other stakeholders who are interested in regularly examining performance at the classroom, department, program, school, or district level. The workbook is structured to help teams and individuals develop *performance indicator systems* that can be used to identify strengths and weaknesses, develop improvement strategies, and monitor progress in meeting education goals.

While the examples in the workbook focus on high schools, elementary and middle schools as well as postsecondary institutions should also find the workbook useful for improving their programs.

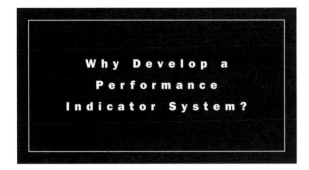

Why Develop a Performance Indicator System?

There are a number of reasons why you should consider developing a performance indicator system at your school:

Take charge of assessing your own performance. Rather than relying on outsiders whose objectives may or may not coincide with your own, you can decide what aspects of performance to monitor, how you will measure that performance, and how you will use the information gathered to guide change.

Identify strengths and weaknesses. Performance indicator data can help you identify both strengths and weaknesses. Strengths can be celebrated and built upon, while weaknesses can be addressed and remedied by developing targeted improvement strategies.

Produce evidence of what improvement strategies are and are not working. Over time, a performance indicator system produces data that enable you to assess whether performance is moving in the direction you expected. If performance is not improving, you can investigate why this is so. Maybe your chosen improvement strategies require a few years to become fully implemented, and performance may be down during the transition period. Maybe certain strategies are ineffective and need to be reevaluated. Or, maybe your school's demographics or other key resources have changed unexpectedly, altering your baseline performance. Performance indicator systems produce data on an ongoing basis, allowing you to monitor trends regularly and to adjust your course as needed.

Disseminate results to better inform the public about student learning and school performance. In addition to using your performance indicator data for internal improvement efforts, you may decide to disseminate some or all of the results. For instance, some schools have developed school report cards that are distributed periodically to teachers, parents, and the school board. By making performance data public, schools demonstrate that they are willing to be held accountable and that they are taking serious, credible steps to improve their performance. Additionally, publicizing performance data can help build support for needed change.

You can reap many benefits from *At Your Fingertips*.

Using Data for Improvement Purposes

At Your Fingertips is designed to help educators use data in new and productive ways. Rather than simply reporting data, you will learn how to use available data for the purpose of improving teaching and learning. Consider the following types of data that are commonly collected by high schools and the different ways in which they are used.

Comparing Reporting and Improvement Purposes		
Data Source	**Reporting Purpose**	**Improvement Purpose**
· Attendance records	· Obtain reimbursement from the state education agency	· Reduce student absences
· Transcripts	· Support student applications to colleges	· Increase on-time graduation · Encourage challenging course taking
· Grades	· Prepare quarterly report cards	· Reduce failure rates
· Test scores	· Meet state requirement to assess students · Develop good public relations	· Assess and modify curriculum and instructional strategies

You may be aware of a number of different data that are collected and maintained at your site and their different purposes.

**Keeping It Simple —
But Informative**

You can learn a lot about performance at your school by paying close attention to everyday data. Data analysis does not have to involve complex statistics. In fact, much can be learned from calculating simple counts, averages, percents, and rates. Consider the national statistics listed below. Although some of these statistics may surprise you, chances are your school collects data that are equally revealing or startling.

Some Typical Data

· An average daily attendance rate of 92 percent means that high school students miss, on average, almost three weeks of school per year.[1]

· About one-quarter (24 percent) of all grades awarded in public high schools are D's and F's.[2]

· Most students (88 percent) hold at least one paid job during their high school years. However, only about 15 percent of high school students obtain a job through a school program or with the help of a teacher or counselor.[3]

· Only about one-third of beginning community college students complete a certificate or degree within four years.[4]

---

[1] On average, 8 percent of public high school students were absent on a typical school day during school year 1993–94. (See U.S. Department of Education 1996a, Supplemental Table 42-1.)

[2] If grades were awarded on a normal or bell curve, you would expect only 16 percent of grades to be D's and F's. The data cited here were derived from the National Education Longitudinal Survey of 1988 and covered students who were in the 9th through 12th grades in 1988–89 to 1991–92.

[3] These statistics were obtained from a representative survey of high school seniors from the class of 1996 in eight states that received federal School-to-Work Opportunities Act implementation grants. (See U.S. Department of Education 1997.)

[4] Specifically, 36.7 percent of beginning students who enrolled in public, 2-year institutions in 1989–90 completed either a certificate (13.4 percent), associate's degree (20.9 percent), or bachelor's degree (2.5 percent) by spring 1994. (See U.S. Department of Education 1996b, Table 3.1.)

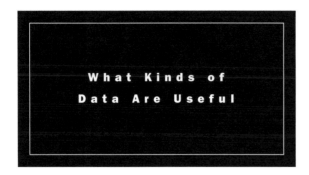

What Kinds of Data Are Useful

By following the steps in this workbook, you will develop performance indicators for key educational outcomes, practices, and inputs that you deem important. Typically, this means you will collect data about such factors as:

· Students

· Staff

· Curriculum

· Instruction

· School climate

· Parent and community relations

The *At Your Fingertips* model, however, is designed to conform to your particular information needs. Instead of collecting a prescribed set of data—or attempting to measure everything that is possibly relevant—you will first decide what your education goals will be and then let these drive your indicator system. Ultimately, the data you collect should provide you with information that is relevant and important to your school's distinct mission and circumstances.

Developing a Performance Indicator System — A Preview

1. Establish goals.

2. Identify related outcomes, practices, and inputs.

3. Determine data sources and indicators.

4. Examine the data.

5. Set performance targets.

6. Monitor performance over time.

This workbook describes a six-step process for establishing a performance indicator system that supports continuous improvement.

These steps are introduced on the following pages and are described in more detail in subsequent chapters.

PIONEER HIGH SCHOOL EXAMPLE

The *At Your Fingertips* workbook periodically visits Pioneer High School (PHS)—a fictitious school that is a composite of several real schools—to illustrate key points. Members of the PHS improvement team introduce each chapter, and PHS examples help clarify important concepts.

On the following pages, the six steps are illustrated using PHS examples. Following each example, you are given the opportunity to think about and examine some preliminary data from your own school.

Developing a Performance Indicator System

THE SIX-STEP AT YOUR FINGERTIPS PROCESS

1 Establish Goals

2 Identify Related Outcomes, Practices, and Inputs

3 Determine Data Sources and Indicators

4 Examine the Data

5 Set Performance Targets

6 Monitor Performance Over Time

STEP 1

ESTABLISH GOALS

Local education goals should drive a performance indicator system. Rather than prescribing a set of data—or attempting to measure everything that might possibly be interesting—the *At Your Fingertips* model focuses your data collection efforts on the information that is most relevant and important to your goals. You are encouraged first to identify what you are striving to achieve, before deciding how to measure whether you are achieving it.

In the *At Your Fingertips* model, goals describe what it is you want students to know, think, believe, value, achieve, or be able to do. These student outcomes are the ultimate objective of schooling.

Examples of goals are provided in the chapter on Step 1.

PIONEER HIGH SCHOOL EXAMPLE

Pioneer High School selected the following as one of its priority goals: "To prepare all students for both further education and meaningful work with advancement possibilities."

This goal is described in fairly broad terms. You may prefer to pursue more targeted goals.

What do you think is most important for your students to know, think, believe, value, achieve, or be able to do?

....

....

....

....

....

....

....

....

....

....

....

....

IDENTIFY RELATED OUTCOMES, PRACTICES, AND INPUTS

In Step 1, you will identify goals that describe what you want for your students. In order to monitor your progress toward achieving these goals, you will need first to clarify the specific outcomes you are interested in monitoring and then to identify the most important practices and inputs that contribute to them. By identifying specific outcomes and related practices and inputs, you will establish a sound performance indicator system that provides a rich source of information for monitoring your school's performance and diagnosing why you are or are not making progress. Ultimately, this step is taken for each goal you identify.

Examples of outcomes, practices, and inputs are provided in the chapter on Step 2.

Defining Outcomes, Practices, and Inputs and Their Relationships

School Practices

Strategies adopted to achieve or improve your targeted student outcomes, including curriculum, instruction, assessment methods, and supporting structures.

Student Outcomes

What you want students to know, think, believe, value, achieve, or be able to do—the ultimate objective of schooling.

School Inputs

Resources you have to work with, including students, staff, community support, physical plant, equipment, and budget. Since many resources are relatively fixed, they are likely to influence the set of practices that are appropriate and the outcomes that are achievable in the short term.

Identifying Specific Outcomes and Related Practices and Inputs

Based on its goal of preparing students for both further education and work, Pioneer High School identified the following specific outcomes and related practices and inputs:

School Practices

· Increase the high school's graduation requirements.

· Provide intensive after-school tutoring services.

· Offer staff development activities on applied academics and integration of academic and vocational education.

· Provide all students with meaningful work-based learning experiences, in particular, job-shadowing, mentoring, and internship opportunities.

Student Outcomes

Goal:

To prepare all students for both further education and meaningful work with advancement possibilities.

Specific Outcomes:

· Attain high academic achievement for all students, especially in English/language arts and mathematics.

· High school graduation.

· Demonstrate work-readiness skills.

School Inputs

· School Board and parent support for increasing high school graduation requirements.

· Availability of staff and volunteers (peers, parents, workplace mentors) to provide after-school tutoring.

· Scheduled common teacher planning time.

· Employer commitment to providing work-based learning experiences.

· Student demographics affecting baseline outcomes (eligibility for free or reduced-price lunch, language spoken in the home, parent educational attainment).

Beginning with one of the goals you described on page 10, first identify the specific outcomes that you want to achieve and then the most important practices and inputs that are related to them.

Identifying Your Specific Outcomes and Related Practices and Inputs

School Practices	Student Outcomes
....	Goal:
....	....
....	....
....	
....	Specific Outcomes:
....	....
....	....
....	....
....	....
....	....
	....

School Inputs

....

....

....

....

....

....

STEP 3

**DETERMINE DATA SOURCES
AND INDICATORS**

Step 3 will help you identify data sources and develop performance indicators for the outcomes, practices, and inputs that you identify in Step 2. *At Your Fingertips* emphasizes using existing data where possible and developing valid, reliable, and fair indicators.

Examples of data sources and indicators are provided in the chapter on Step 3.

Defining Data Sources and Indicators

For each outcome, practice, and input you should determine . . .

Priority Data Sources

Broadly conceived, data include all of the information and records that your school routinely collects. Relevant information may be

· Maintained in an automated, centralized computer system;

· Maintained centrally, but kept as paper records in a filing cabinet; or

· Decentralized, for example, maintained by individual teachers in their classrooms.

Data sources can be either formal and standardized, or informal and ad hoc. In some cases, you may develop targeted new data sources.

Corresponding Performance Indicators

Performance indicators are statistics that help measure progress on your outcomes, practices, and inputs. Indicators are usually expressed as

· Counts,

· Averages,

· Percents, or

· Rates.

The process of developing performance indicators helps you define your education goals and transform vague goals into measurable ones.

Determining Data Sources and Indicators

Based on the specific outcomes and related practices and inputs it identified in Step 2, Pioneer High School decided to use the following data sources and indicators. See page 12 for descriptions of their outcomes, practices, and inputs.

1. Outcomes

Priority Data Sources	Corresponding Performance Indicators
· Achievement test scores	· Average reading, mathematics, and science scores on state tests
· Student transcripts	· Percent of graduating seniors meeting the state university's entrance requirements
· Guidance records	· High school graduation rate
· Employer evaluations	· Percent of seniors participating in work-based learning experiences who received a satisfactory or higher rating from employers

2. Practices

Priority Data Sources	Corresponding Performance Indicators
· Program of studies	· Minimum number of credits in core academic subject areas required for graduation
· Tutoring sign-in sheets	· Number of students participating at least 1) once a semester and 2) once a week
· Staff development records	· Number of teachers attending in-services on integrating academic and vocational education
· Teacher survey	· Percent of participating teachers reporting they have collaborated with other teachers to develop integrated lesson plans
· School-to-work liaison records	· Percent of graduating seniors who participated in an organized work-based learning experience

3. Inputs

Priority Data Sources	Corresponding Performance Indicators
· Guidance records	· Number of hours logged by staff and volunteers to provide tutoring
· Master schedule	· Number of minutes per week of scheduled common teacher planning time
· School-to-work liaison records	· Number of work-based learning openings for 1) job shadowing, 2) mentoring, and 3) internships
· Guidance records	· Percent of students 1) eligible for free or reduced-price lunch, 2) who speak a language other than English at home, and 3) whose parent(s) completed a college degree

Determining Your Data Sources and Indicators

Referring back to the specific outcomes and related practices and inputs you identified on page 13, determine the priority data sources and corresponding performance indicators you can use to monitor your outcomes, practices, and inputs.

1. Outcomes

Priority Data Sources	Corresponding Performance Indicators
....	....
....	....
....	....
....	....

2. Practices

Priority Data Sources	Corresponding Performance Indicators
....	....
....	....
....	....
....	....

3. Inputs

Priority Data Sources	Corresponding Performance Indicators
....	....
....	....
....	....
....	....

STEP 4

EXAMINE THE DATA

After identifying data sources, developing performance indicators, and reviewing those indicators for validity, reliability, and fairness, you are ready to gather, examine, and interpret your baseline data. Step 4 offers tips for understanding what your data are telling you about how you are performing on your goals. The chapter introduces several techniques for interpreting data, cautions against common pitfalls, and offers alternate ways of presenting your findings.

Pioneer High School created an annual school report card to help stakeholders monitor their progress in meeting the education goals selected by PHS. The school's baseline data are described in the column for academic year 1993–94. Performance targets are established as part of Step 5.

Selected Performance Indicators	1993–1994	1994–1995	1995–1996	Percent Change	Performance Target
1. Targeted Student Outcomes					
Average reading score on the state achievement test*	265	267	269	+1.5%	350
Average mathematics score on the state achievement test*	278	285	289	+4.0%	350
Average science score on the state achievement test*	257	258	257	+0%	350
Percent of graduating seniors meeting the state university's entrance requirements**	47%	45%	43%	-8.5%	95%
High school graduation rate	88%	89%	90%	+2.3%	95%
Percent of seniors participating in work-based learning experiences who received a satisfactory or higher rating from employers	80%	80%	87%	+8.8%	100%
2. Related School Practices					
Minimum number of credits in core academic subject areas required for graduation**	10	10	10	0%	13
Number of students participating in tutoring services:***					
·At least once a semester	263	380	442	+68%	1000
·At least once a week	21	42	53	+152%	100
Number of teachers attending in-services on integrating academic and vocational education	20	35	45	+125%	67
Percent of participating teachers reporting they have collaborated with other teachers to develop integrated lesson plans during the last year	50%	71%	76%	+52%	100%
Percent of graduating seniors who participated in an organized work-based learning experience	2%	6%	30%	+1400%	100%
3. Related School Inputs					
Number of hours logged to provide tutoring by:					
·Staff	870	1850	1780	+105%	1800
·Volunteers	320	600	885	+177%	1200
Number of minutes per week of scheduled common teacher planning time	45	225	225	+400%	225
Number of work-based learning openings for:					
·Job shadowing (10th grade)	75	75	100	+33%	250
·Mentoring (11th grade)	15	25	35	+233%	125
·Internships (12th grade)	5	10	20	+400%	75
Percent of students:					
·Eligible for subsidized lunches	43%	45%	47%	+9.3%	N/A
·Who speak a language other than English at home	20%	21%	22%	+10%	N/A
·Whose parent(s) completed a college degree	25%	23%	20%	-20%	N/A

*Scoring scale: Basic (250), Proficient (300), Advanced (350).
**PHS increased its high school graduation requirements in 1993 for students who will graduate in 1997 and after.
***Over time, performance on this indicator might be expected to decline.

As a preview of what lies ahead, you may find it interesting to gather any data you have on the performance indicators you identified in Step 3. Space has been provided below to fill in baseline data for your classroom, department, program, school, or district. You will fill in the trend data and performance targets in later steps.

Classroom/Department/Program/School/District: _____

Selected Performance Indicators	Baseline Data (year)	Trend Data (year)	Trend Data (year)	Performance Targets
(copy your indicators from page 16)	_____	_____	_____	
1. Targeted Student Outcomes				
2. Related School Practices				
3. Related School Inputs				

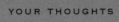
After reviewing your baseline performance on the indicators you have selected, record your first impressions below.

1. In what areas are you performing well?

....

....

....

2. What areas appear to need improvement?

....

....

....

3. What questions, if any, do these data raise for you?

....

....

....

4. What additional information do you need to understand your indicator data better?

....

....

....

STEP 5

SET PERFORMANCE TARGETS

Step 5 helps you set performance targets—the level of performance you will strive for on your indicators. Setting targets involves deciding how satisfied you are with your current performance, specifying the levels of performance you want to achieve, and then devising strategies to achieve them. Performance targets are specific and measurable. If your goals were not measurable in their original form in Step 1, they should be after you set targets in this step.

There are four main sources of information on appropriate performance targets. You can . . .

· Review relevant state and national performance standards.

· Discuss expectations with important stakeholder groups.

· Compare your performance with that of an exemplary school or program.

· Compare your performance with state and national averages.

Seeking information from multiple sources is a good strategy for setting challenging and realistic performance targets.

PIONEER HIGH SCHOOL EXAMPLE

Pioneer High School's performance targets are listed in the final column of their report card on page 18.

Think about where you can obtain information on performance targets for the indicators you listed in your report card on page 19.

1. What types of educational performance standards are being used in your state or locality?

....

....

....

2. What local stakeholder groups could contribute information on appropriate performance levels for your high school students?

....

....

....

3. Among your peer institutions, which schools or programs are known for their exemplary performance?

....

....

....

4. What data are available to compare schools or programs in your state?

....

....

....

After thinking about the above sources of information, you may want to investigate some of them. Then, you may want to return to the mock report card on page 19 to fill in your preliminary performance targets.

MONITOR PERFORMANCE
OVER TIME

Step 6 helps you make your indicator system part of an ongoing and systematic improvement process. The chapter helps you organize data collection and monitoring efforts, interpret trend data, and improve your data sources and indicators.

After working through the six steps, you may want to return from time to time to earlier steps. Performance data sometimes raise as many questions as they answer. Such is the nature of continuous improvement. Developing an indicator system requires a certain amount of trial and error, and it is unlikely that you will identify all of the most relevant and appropriate information on the first try. However, the strength of performance indicator systems is that they ultimately guide improvement efforts based on objective—if imperfect—data, rather than on hunches, anecdotal evidence, fads, or historical practices.

PIONEER HIGH SCHOOL EXAMPLE

Pioneer High School's report card on page 18 tracked performance on its indicators over three years.

If you have trend data on any of your performance indicators, you may want to fill in the appropriate columns in the mock report card on page 19.

1. Are there apparent trends in any of your student outcome indicators? If so, what are they? If you do not have trend data, what is your general impression of how students have performed on your outcome indicators in recent years?

....

....

2. Why do you think performance is headed in this direction?

....

....

3. Do you have any practice or input data to back up your hypotheses?

....

....

4. What additional information do you need to investigate further?

....

....

5. What practices or strategies—that are already in place at your school—do you think will improve performance on your indicators over time?

....

....

6. What additional strategies might you adopt to improve performance on your indicators?

....

....

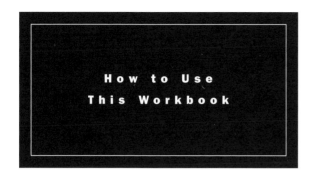

How to Use This Workbook

The *At Your Fingertips* workbook explains how you can develop a performance indicator system that supports continuous improvement. The workbook describes important concepts, offers many examples, provides space for you to record your own thoughts as you read, and includes worksheets at the end of each chapter to move you step by step toward establishing your indicator system.

The workbook material is equally relevant for individuals who want to examine the quality of teaching and learning in their own classrooms or departments and for teams of teachers, administrators, and other stakeholders who want to monitor the performance of an entire program, school, or district. Teams should work together on the worksheets and can prepare for an upcoming meeting by reading the relevant chapters ahead of time. Individuals can work at their own pace. While some of the worksheets mention group activities, individuals can also do these on their own. Black-and-white versions of the worksheets are provided (for photocopying purposes) at the conclusion of the workbook.

If you decide to work as a team, you are encouraged to designate a facilitator for each team meeting. Important decisions about improvement efforts may be made at these meetings. A facilitator can ensure that the worksheets are completed, keep track of time, help the team reach consensus, record final group decisions, and make copies of the completed worksheets for the project files. Since you will often refer back to previously completed worksheets, it is important that you maintain complete and well-organized project files.

NEXT STEPS

You are now ready to start developing a comprehensive performance indicator system.
The next chapter—Getting Started—explains why it is advantageous to consider taking a team approach to developing your performance indicator system and offers guidelines for doing so. The chapter also identifies some important logistical and scheduling considerations for teams and individuals alike.

Getting Started

This chapter helps you assemble a team of education stakeholders for the purpose of developing a performance indicator system that supports continuous improvement. The chapter explains why a team approach is worthwhile and describes steps for building a team that suits your unique needs. Persons working alone are also encouraged to read this chapter, or you may want to skip forward to Step 1. All of the remaining chapters are equally useful for both individual and collaborative efforts to improve schooling.

"My son is a 10th grader at Pioneer High School. When I received a letter from Dr. Wilson inviting me to be a member of the school improvement team, I wasn't sure how I could contribute, but I decided to go to the orientation meeting anyway. Am I ever glad I did! The PHS teachers and administrators have been very welcoming, and I've learned a lot about the challenges the school faces and how committed the staff are. I also feel I've been able to make a valuable contribution. As a team, we decided that one of the goals we wanted for our school was to get more parents involved in their children's education. Although we brainstormed together about ways to involve parents, the teachers and administrators really looked to the parents to give them a 'reality' check about the best strategies. They also seemed truly interested in hearing our ideas about the education goals we have for our children. Since my son has a learning disability, I wanted to make sure that the goals and improvement strategies the team adopted kept students with special needs in mind. All in all, the performance indicator project has been a stimulating and heartening experience."

Mrs. Jane Gibson — Parent

Improving education in your district, school, or program is not a one-person job. It requires many people working together to achieve the same goals. In many cases, administrators initiate reform efforts. However, teachers must implement most reforms, and students must respond to them. Having parents embrace reforms can also make a significant difference. To ensure that your school prepares students for their futures, it also helps to seek the advice and support of employers who hire graduates and the postsecondary institutions that enroll them. These stakeholders and others can contribute important perspectives to improvement efforts.

A good guiding principle when thinking about team membership is that all groups who will be responsible for implementing improvement efforts or who will have a stake in the results should either be represented on the team or serve as consultants. It is also helpful to strike a balance between involving a large number of participants and building a team capable of working together productively.

"Good schools do not encourage silent partners."

RENIHAN AND RENIHAN 1989

Broad participation in improvement efforts serves to . . .

- Promote a high level of support for your efforts.

- Generate sound solutions by expanding the discussion.

- Motivate participants and their associates.

- Increase the likelihood that the effort will lead to constructive action.

- Prepare participants for their role in implementing improvements.

- Increase ownership of and commitment to specific strategies.

- Empower important stakeholder groups.

- Foster lasting, rather than temporary, change.

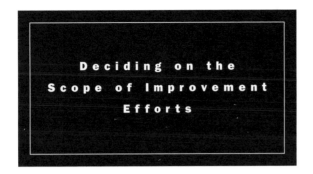

Deciding on the Scope of Improvement Efforts

A first step in building a team is deciding what the scope of improvement efforts will be. Are you interested in developing a districtwide improvement process where participants establish common goals and strategies for the entire district, possibly in addition to complementary goals and strategies for each school? Or are you interested in developing a school-based improvement process that focuses on a single school and involves a cross-section of stakeholders from that school? As a third option, you may be interested in developing an improvement process for a particular program within your school or one that is common to several schools, such as writing across the curriculum or tech-prep, involving a subset of stakeholders at each site. Departments or individual teachers might choose to create an improvement process focusing on the specific issues facing them in their departments and classrooms, such as poor attendance, low achievement, or discipline problems. Before assembling an improvement team, you will need to decide what scope of effort is best for you:

· District

· School

· Program

· Department

· Classroom

A districtwide effort that involves several schools will usually require a larger team than a school-based or program-specific improvement effort. For simplicity's sake, this workbook refers to "school" improvement.

Lay the groundwork by selecting a team of education stakeholders.

Establishing an Improvement Team

In this chapter, it is assumed that you will either organize a new team or modify the composition or purpose of an existing group to take responsibility for developing your performance indicator system that supports continuous improvement.

"Change — no matter how positive the outcome — cannot be imposed from above. Those who will feel the impact of the change must be involved from the beginning."

SOUTHERN REGIONAL EDUCATION BOARD (SREB), *HIGH SCHOOLS THAT WORK* NETWORK (1995)

Although it may be known by a different name, you may already have a committee or group at your school that is responsible for improvement efforts. For example, a group may be in charge of strategic planning for your district or school, or a steering committee may be responsible for implementing a new program. As you work through this chapter, you will need to consider:

- Whether your district, school, program, or department already has an appropriate committee in place and has no need to create a new group.

- Whether the improvement team you establish through this workbook should combine with a preexisting committee, be a subset of that committee, or be an adjunct to it.

- What the similarities and differences are between the different groups' responsibilities.

- How best to communicate with a preexisting group to avoid working at cross-purposes or duplicating efforts.

Identifying Potential Team Members

Below is a list of stakeholder groups that you may want to consider involving in your improvement team. You will find more detailed descriptions of how these persons can contribute to improvement efforts in Appendix A. Selecting members for your team will require deciding which stakeholder groups are vital to your improvement efforts and which are less essential.

Important Stakeholder Groups

- Students
- Parents
- Teachers
- Department chairpersons
- Career or guidance counselors

- Principals and other school administrators
- Other school staff
- Superintendents and other district administrators
- School board members
- Union leaders

- State or regional education agency staff
- Employers
- Postsecondary education representatives
- Other community leaders

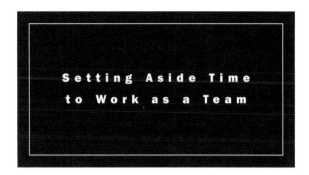

**Setting Aside Time
to Work as a Team**

You may be wondering how long it will take to establish a performance indicator system at your school. In order to complete the activities in this workbook, your team will need to meet for a minimum of 32 hours. One way to do this would be to schedule a regular four-hour monthly meeting over the course of an entire academic year. A more intensive approach would involve meeting for 16 hours one week, and then meeting another 16 hours about four to six weeks later. (You will need some time between Steps 3 and 4 to gather baseline data.) Clearly, there are many ways to plan your team meetings. However, because the workbook covers what is often unfamiliar material, most participants find that four hours is the maximum amount of time they can meet and be productive on a single day.

In addition to the 32 hours of meeting time, team members will also need to prepare for meetings by reading the relevant workbook chapters ahead of time. In some cases, teams will establish task forces to develop new data sources or specific improvement strategies. This task force time will be over and above the standard meeting time. Once the groundwork has been laid, however, you will need much less time to monitor your progress in future years.

The calendar on the following two pages offers a possible schedule for establishing your performance indicator system and monitoring your performance over time. The schedule follows the academic year, with team members meeting for approximately 32 hours during Year 1, and then for about 12 hours in subsequent years. While some schools find it easiest to follow the academic calendar, it is not necessary to do so. You may begin using this workbook at any time. For example, your school may prefer to take advantage of the summer months preceding or following the academic year to complete many of the workbook activities. The following is only a suggested calendar to give you a sense of the time commitment that team members will be asked to make.

September	October	November	December
Introduction and Getting Started Readers become familiar with the *At Your Fingertips* process by reading the first two chapters. Invite stakeholders to join your team.	**Getting Started** Hold an orientation and organizational meeting for potential team members (two hours).	**Step 1 — Establish Goals** Team meets for goal-setting session (four hours).	**Step 2 — Identify Related Outcomes, Practices, and Inputs** Team meets to identify specific outcomes and related practices and inputs (four hours).

January	February	March	April
Step 3 — Determine Data Sources and Indicators Team meets to identify data sources and develop indicators (four hours).	Responsible persons gather existing data identified in the previous workshop (data are collected over four to six weeks).	**Step 4 — Examine the Data** Team meets to review the data (four hours).	**Step 5 — Set Performance Targets** Team meets to set performance targets (four hours).

May	June	July	August
Step 6 — Monitor Performance Over Time Team meets to assign roles and establish a timeline for disseminating performance data and implementing improvement efforts (four hours).	Task forces meet to prepare the first performance report, develop new data sources, and work on improvement strategies.	Task forces meet as necessary.	Task forces meet as necessary.

GETTING STARTED

September	October	November	December
School publishes previous year's performance report.	Team meets to review previous year's data, confirm schedule for implementing improvement strategies and collecting data, and possibly revise goals and indicators (four hours). Review Workbook.	Task forces meet as necessary.	Task forces meet as necessary.

January	February	March	April
Task forces meet as necessary.	If the team wants to collect data each semester, responsible persons gather indicator data for the fall semester at this time (data are collected over four to six weeks).	Team meets to review any fall semester data (four hours). Review Steps 4–6.	School publishes fall semester performance report.

May	June	July	August
Team meets to assign roles and confirm a timeline for disseminating performance data and implementing improvement efforts (four hours).	Task forces meet to prepare the spring or annual performance report, develop new data sources, and work on improvement strategies (four hours).	Task forces meet as necessary.	Task forces meet as necessary.

Worksheets GS1 and GS2 will help you organize your team:

GS1 — Identifying Team Members

Helps you identify important stakeholder groups and

individuals. The person who is responsible for launching the performance indicator system at your school should fill out this worksheet before convening the first team meeting.

A sample invitation letter is included in Appendix B.

GS2 — Organizing Your Team

Helps you establish basic organizational guidelines. Team members should complete the worksheet at the first meeting.

A sample meeting agenda is included in Appendix C.

You can begin building an improvement team by completing the four activities that follow. The individual who is responsible for launching a performance indicator system at your school should fill out the worksheet before convening the first team meeting.

1. Decide what the scope of your improvement efforts will primarily be. Select one area for improvement, and then identify the district(s), school(s), program(s), department(s), or classroom(s) you hope will participate:

☐ District ....

☐ School ....

☐ Program ....

☐ Department ....

☐ Classroom ....

2. Who should be represented on your team? Check (√) all groups that apply, and list key individuals from each group who should be invited:

☐ Students ....

☐ Parents ....

☐ Teachers ....

☐ Department chairpersons ....

☐ Career or guidance counselors ....

☐ School administrators ....

☐ Other school staff ....

☐ District administrators ....

☐ School Board members ....

☐ Union leaders ....

☐ State education agency staff ....

☐ Employers ....

☐ Postsecondary education representatives ....

☐ Other community members ....

3. Who should be the team leader? ....

4. An invitation letter, conversation, or phone call should do the following things: (Space has been provided for you to jot down notes about what you might include in your invitation, and a sample invitation letter is included in Appendix B.)

Alert the reader to the upcoming project to develop a performance indicator system.

What will you call the project? ....

How can you get their attention? ....

Explain the need for the project.

....

....

Explain the benefits of being involved.

....

....

Briefly describe the project.

....

....

Describe the time commitment team members will be expected to make.

....

....

Specify the date, time, and location of an orientation and organizational meeting.

....

....

Explain the next step that prospective team members should take to demonstrate their interest.

....

....

You may want to enclose a copy of the Introduction along with the invitation letter to provide prospective participants with more information about the improvement process.

This worksheet should be completed by participants at the first team meeting. You can begin organizing your improvement team by completing the following five activities:

1. Use the space below to note any questions that you would like answered during the orientation and organizational meeting. Record responses to those questions as they arise.

....

....

....

....

2. Are there any stakeholder groups or persons missing from the meeting who would be a valuable addition to the team? Use the space below to identify them.

....

....

....

....

3. Discuss and record who will assume the following roles and responsibilities for your team:

Role	Person Responsible
Meeting facilitator (guides participants as they fill out the worksheets and discuss important issues)	....
Archivist (keeps copies of completed worksheets and other documentation)	....
Meeting organizer (reserves meeting room, sends reminders)	....
Other role	....
Other role	....

4. Decide when and where your improvement team will meet. You may want to refer to the suggested calendar for Year 1 on page 33 of this chapter for ideas.

· How frequently will the team meet? ....

· About how long will team meetings last? ....

· When will the next meeting be held (date and time)? ....

· Where will the next meeting be held? ....

· Does anything else need to happen before the next meeting? If so, what? Who will be responsible? ....

....

....

....

Team members should plan to read the chapter *Step 1—Establishing Goals* before the next meeting.

5. Determine what your team ground rules and operating procedures will be. As a group, discuss and answer the following questions:

· How will team decisions be finalized (consensus, voting, other)?

....

....

· How will team members communicate with each other (meetings, memos, e-mail, other)?

....

....

· How will team members communicate with non-members (staff meetings, newsletter, other)?

....

....

· Other rules or procedures? ....

....

....

NEXT STEPS

You may want to file copies of Worksheets GS1 and GS2 for
future reference, in case questions come up about who will be on your
improvement team and how it will be organized.

You are now ready to work together as a team to establish a set of education
goals that will form the foundation of your performance indicator system.

Step 1 | Establish Goals

Step 1 helps you establish a set of education goals that will form the foundation of your performance indicator system and continuous improvement efforts. If your school has already established goals, this chapter will help you review those goals and set priorities among them.

"I've been teaching electronics at Pioneer High School for 12 years. Most of that time I've spent in my lab in the vocational wing of the school. This project marks the first time I've worked closely with such a large group of teachers, administrators, and others. It's also the first time we've all discussed what we want for our students. · It's surprising how much our team sees eye to eye. Everyone is concerned about students' academic achievement, their being prepared for the adult world, and their making positive contributions to society. Sometimes our specific concerns differ, but most importantly, we agree about the general direction we should be moving in. · Each team member has had something unique to contribute. I think I helped some people understand what we're trying to do in vocational education and how the study of electronics overlaps with other subjects. I also learned a lot listening to other team members' concerns. All in all, I think we've come up with a solid set of goals from working together."

Mr. Joe Greene — Electronics Teacher, Pioneer High School

· ·

Beginning
With Goals

Local education goals should drive a performance indicator system. Rather than prescribing a set of data—or attempting to measure everything that might possibly be interesting—the *At Your Fingertips* model focuses your data collection efforts on the information that is most relevant and important to your goals. You are encouraged first to identify what you are striving to achieve, before deciding how to measure whether you

are achieving it. If performance indicators are not rooted in goals, the indicators themselves may become the de facto goals, and improving the data—rather than the underlying performance—may become an end in itself.

What Do You Want for Your Students?

Public education exists to foster and support the intellectual growth and social development of students. This chapter helps you make decisions about the specific goals you want to serve as the focus of your performance indicator system.

In the *At Your Fingertips* model, goals describe what you want students to know, think, believe, value, achieve, or be able to do. These student outcomes are the ultimate objective of schooling.

Sow the seeds for your indicator system by establishing education goals.

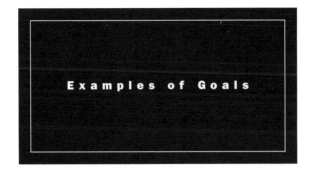

Examples of Goals

Some examples of goals from national and state school reform initiatives are provided below. You may agree with these goals or have very different ideas about what goals will best serve your community. These examples serve only as illustrations.

· "[T]o teach for understanding; to prepare individuals for the world beyond school; to develop each person's potential fully; to make sure that students master core knowledge ..." (examples of goals cited by Howard Gardner [September 1997, p. 20]).

· "Every public school student shall master the basic skills and knowledge necessary for (1) managing the dual roles of family member and wage earner; and (2) gaining entry-level employment in a high-skill, high-wage job, or continuing the student's education at the post-secondary level" (Senate Bill 1 of the 74th Texas Legislature, sec. 29.181, established for career and technology education).

· "Each student masters a limited number of essential skills and areas of knowledge. While these skills and areas will, to varying degrees, reflect the traditional academic disciplines, the program's design should be shaped by the intellectual and imaginative powers and competencies that students need, rather than by 'subjects' as conventionally defined" (A Common Principle of the *Coalition of Essential Schools* [see Sizer 1989]).

· "To increase the mathematics, science, and communication achievement of students in general and vocational programs to the national average by the year 2000" (Southern Regional Education Board's *High Schools That Work* network [see Bottoms and Mikos 1995]).

· "By the year 2000, the high school graduation rate will increase to at least 90 percent" (1994 Goals 2000 Act).

PIONEER HIGH SCHOOL EXAMPLE

Pioneer High School selected the following as one of its priority goals:
"To prepare all students for both further education and meaningful work with advancement possibilities."

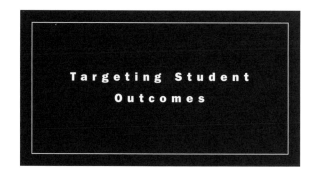

Targeting Student Outcomes

As the preceding examples illustrate, goals can vary in purpose and form. For example, some goals provide a broad vision for education reform, while others are written in more narrow terms and may even specify a numerical performance target. Some goals pertain to all students in a school or school system, while others pertain to a subset of students in a particular program, such as a vocational education or career and technology education program.

Nevertheless, all of the goals in the preceding examples target student outcomes, which drive the school improvement process. Some reform initiatives may also seek to change particular school practices (for example, curriculum, instruction, assessment methods, and supporting structures), or even school inputs (resources you have to work with, including students, staff, community support, physical plant, equipment, and budget). You may have some goals at your school that describe school practices or inputs rather than student outcomes. However, it is important to be clear about the student outcomes you are striving to achieve through these practices and inputs. The *At Your Fingertips* model helps you keep your school practices and inputs focused on the ultimate objective—student learning. Step 2 will provide you with the opportunity to examine the relationship between outcomes, practices, and inputs more closely.

**Locating
Existing Goals**

Your school may already have established some goals. Sometimes goals are formed as part of other education initiatives. For example, your school may have identified goals when it undertook strategic planning, conducted a community needs assessment, developed a new program, or implemented a new curriculum. Your school may also have identified goals in order to satisfy various grant application requirements or may have been asked to adopt national, state, or district goals.

YOUR THOUGHTS

1. Has your district, school, program, or department already established goals? If so, what are they?

....

....

....

....

....

....

2. What do you want your students to know, think, believe, value, achieve, or be able to do?

....

....

....

....

....

....

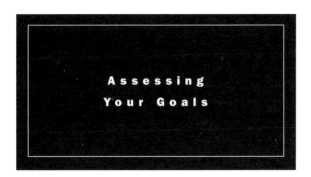

Assessing Your Goals

Whether reviewing and revising existing goals or establishing new ones, you will be asked to assess your goals according to the criteria listed below. These criteria help ensure that your selected goals will be effective in bringing about the change you desire.

Goals should be...

1. Meaningful

2. Realistic

3. Complementary

4. Given clear priorities

5. Agreed to by all stakeholders

6. Measurable

Adapted from Stecher and Hanser (1992).

1. A goal is *meaningful* if its meaning is clear to all stakeholders and it produces something of educational value.

2. A goal is *realistic* if you can feasibly achieve it over time.

3. Goals are *complementary* if they contribute to your overall vision. Any goal that conflicts with others should be reexamined.

4. Because limited resources may prevent you from pursuing all goals simultaneously or with equal attention, you should set *clear priorities* among your goals.

5. *All persons who have a stake in the education process or who will be responsible for helping to achieve the goals should be familiar with and support them.*

6. A goal is *measurable* if it specifies the level of performance that is expected or a numerical target. Your team will set performance targets in Step 5.[5]

[5] Some evaluators encourage establishing measurable goals up front—that is, goals that specify numerical targets. In some cases, this emphasis on measurement may be premature and force you to adopt arbitrary targets. The *At Your Fingertips* model encourages you to collect baseline data and gather information on performance standards before setting your numerical targets. By working through the six steps in this workbook, you should transform your original goals into measurable ones.

STEP

Establish Goals

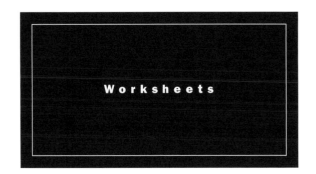

Worksheets

Worksheets 1.1–1.3 will help you establish a set of education goals that form the foundation of your performance indicator system and continuous improvement efforts.[6] Although the worksheets are designed for teams, individuals can complete the activities on their own.

First, you should determine whether your district, school, program, or department already has existing goals to work with. If you do, begin with Worksheet 1.2. If not, begin with Worksheet 1.1.

1.1 — Establishing New Goals

Helps you establish a set of education goals, if you do not already have any.

1.2 — Reviewing and Revising Existing Goals

Helps you review and revise existing goals.

1.3 — Setting Priorities Among Your Goals

Helps you set priorities among your goals.

[6] The process outlined in Worksheets 1.1 and 1.2 was adapted from the National Study of School Evaluation (1993), and M. Dutton et al. (1994).

Activities 1–9 in this worksheet will help you establish a set of education goals, for those who do not already have existing goals or who want to start the goal-setting process over again. (If you already have goals you would like to consider, skip to Worksheet 1.2.) If you are working as part of a team, your entire team should plan to complete this worksheet together in order to reach consensus on your goals.

1. Display or distribute copies of the following six criteria: "Goals should be meaningful, realistic, complementary, given clear priorities, agreed to by all stakeholders, and measurable."

2. As a **large group**, review the examples of goals provided on page 44. Goals should focus on student outcomes—what it is you want students to know, think, believe, value, achieve, or be able to do. Goals may be written in broad or specific terms, and may focus on all students or a subset of students.

3. **Individually**, think about what you believe are the most important education goals for your district, school, program, department, or classroom. Your goals should describe desired student outcomes. Record your ideas in the space below:

· ·

4. Break up into **small groups** of three to five persons to share the goals you identified in Activity 3. Ask yourselves the following question: Which of these goals do we all value for our students? Record areas of agreement and disagreement below. If you have a long list of agreed-upon goals, check off the 10 goals that your small group considers most important, and designate a spokesperson who will describe these goals to the large group.

· ·

5. Everyone returns to the **large group**. The designated spokesperson from each small group shares his or her group's goals (including areas of agreement and disagreement) with the large group. Then the large group identifies and discusses themes that are common among all the groups, and the facilitator records them and lists the different goal statements that fall under each theme. You may need to weed out some goals that do not focus on student outcomes.

6. Break up into different **small groups** of three to five persons (mixing up the membership of previous groups). The facilitator then assigns one or more thematic areas to each group, so that all themes are assigned. In your small group, review your theme and the related goal ideas, and then draft one or more goal statements to summarize your thematic area. Designate a spokesperson for your group.

Your small group's theme(s): ....

....

....

....

....

Summary goal statement(s): ....

....

....

....

....

7. Everyone returns to the **large group**. The designated spokesperson from each small group shares his or her group's goal statements with the large group. The facilitator then records the goal statements and displays them where everyone can see them.

8. As a **large group**, team members discuss any differences of opinions that may have come up over goal selection or wording and attempt to agree on a common set of goals.

9. In the space provided below, write down the final agreed-upon goal statement(s) for your small group's thematic area. The facilitator should record all of the final goal statements so they are available for future use.

Final goal statement(s) for your thematic area: ....

....

....

....

....

....

....

➡️ **Proceed to Worksheet 1.3**

Activities 1–9 in this worksheet help you review and revise your existing education goals. (If you do not have any existing goals, return to Worksheet 1.1.) If you are working as part of a team, your entire team should plan to complete this worksheet together in order to reach consensus on your goals. Before beginning the worksheet, your meeting facilitator should collect all sets of education goals that have already been established at your school. Goals may have been developed as part of other education initiatives, such as strategic planning efforts, conducting a community needs assessment, developing a new program, implementing a new curriculum, or as part of a grant application process.

1. Display or distribute copies of the following six criteria: "Goals should be meaningful, realistic, complementary, given clear priorities, agreed to by all stakeholders, and measurable."

2. As a **large group**, review the examples of goals provided on page 44. Goals should focus on student outcomes—what it is you want students to know, think, believe, value, achieve, or be able to do. Goals may be written in broad or specific terms, and may focus on all students or a subset of students.

3. Display or distribute copies of your school's existing goals.

4. Break up into **small groups** of three to five persons to review the existing goals. First, identify the goals that describe student outcomes, and focus on these. Then, ask yourselves the following questions:

   · Which of these goals do we value most?

   · Are there any goals that are less important?

   · Are there any important goals that are missing?

   Record areas of agreement and disagreement below. If you have a long list of agreed-upon goals, check off the 10 goals that your small group considers most important, and designate a spokesperson who will describe them to the large group.

5. Everyone returns to the **large group**. The designated spokesperson from each small group shares his or her group's modified goals (including areas of agreement and disagreement) with the large group. The large group then identifies and discusses themes that were common among all the groups. The facilitator writes down these themes and lists the different goal statements that fall under each theme. You may need to weed out some goals that do not focus on student outcomes.

6. Break up into different **small groups** of three to five persons (mixing up the membership of previous groups). The facilitator assigns one or more thematic areas to each group, so that all themes are assigned. In your small group, review your theme and its related goals, and then draft one or more goal statements to summarize your thematic area. You may decide that the original goal statement was adequate, or you may want to revise the statement or combine several statements into a single new statement. Designate a spokesperson for your group.

Your small group's theme(s): ....

....

....

....

....

Revised goal statement(s): ....

....

....

....

....

7. Everyone returns to the **large group**. The designated spokesperson from each small group shares his or her group's goal statements with the large group. The facilitator then records the goal statements and displays them where everyone can see them.

8. As a **large group**, team members discuss any differences of opinions that may have come up over goal selection or wording and attempt to agree on a common set of goals.

9. In the space below, write down the final agreed-upon goal statement(s) for your small group's thematic area. The facilitator should record all of the final goals so they are available for future use.

Final goal statement(s) for your thematic area: ....

....

....

....

....

....

➪ **Proceed to Worksheet 1.3**

After completing either Worksheet 1.1 or 1.2, you are ready to assess your goals based on the six criteria described in this chapter; revise or eliminate any problematic goals; and then set priorities among the remaining ones. Limited resources may prevent you from pursuing all goals simultaneously or with equal effort, or may require you to phase in data collection efforts. Moreover, starting small may be a better strategy for success than tackling all of your goals at once. Delineating clear goal priorities at the outset will help your team organize its improvement efforts.

1. Display or distribute copies of the final goal statements that your team agreed upon when completing Worksheet 1.1 or 1.2. As a **large group**, review the goal statements by discussing the questions listed below. Flag any goal statements that do not meet the following criteria:

· Is the *meaning* of the goals clear? Will the goals yield something of educational value?

· ·

· ·

· Can the goals *realistically* be achieved over time?

· ·

· ·

· Do the goals *contribute* to an overall vision? Does any goal conflict with the others?

· ·

· ·

· Have the goals been *agreed upon* by most team members? By the larger education community? If not, what steps should be taken to obtain broad consensus?

· ·

· ·

· Think for a moment about budget, staffing, or political constraints at your site. Should any goals be more or less of a *priority* than others based on these constraints?

· ·

· ·

· Can you foresee how you might *measure* progress toward achieving the goals? Will it be possible to establish a performance target for each goal? (It is not necessary to set the actual targets at this time.)

· ·

· ·

2. As a **large group**, reexamine any goals that you flagged in Step 1. You may choose either to eliminate or revise a problematic goal. If you decide to revise any of the goals, record the revised goal statements in the space below.

....

....

....

....

....

3. Goals that meet the six criteria described in this chapter should receive higher priority than those that do not. As a **large group**, discuss which goals should receive top priority, beginning with priority number one.

4. Record your final goal statements in priority order below. (It will help you focus your efforts if you have no more than 10 priority goals.)

1. ....

....

2. ....

....

3. ....

....

4. ....

....

5. ....

....

6. ....

....

7. ....

....

8. ....

....

9. ....

....

10. ....

....

NEXT STEPS

Be sure to file a completed copy of Worksheet 1.3 for future reference.

You are now ready to identify
the related outcomes, practices, and inputs you will eventually measure.

Step 2 | Identify Related Outcomes, Practices, and Inputs

In Step 1, you identified goals that describe what you want for your students. In order to monitor your progress toward achieving these goals, you will first need to clarify the specific outcomes you are interested in monitoring and then identify the most important practices and inputs that are related to them. By identifying specific outcomes and related practices and inputs, you will be on your way to establishing a sound performance indicator system that provides a rich source of information for monitoring your performance and diagnosing why you are or are not making progress.

"As a junior at Pioneer High School, I don't have many chances to work closely on school projects with teachers, counselors, and administrators, so the performance indicator project taught me a lot. Step 2 helped me become aware of different things that affect my grades in school—things that I never really thought mattered. Since I usually listen in class, take notes, do my homework, and study the night before quizzes and tests, I've done pretty well during high school and get decent grades. When I said this during a team meeting, everyone seemed surprised. They kept asking me questions, wanting me to explain more about what I just said. One teacher asked if I thought *any* of my classes were difficult. I told him that math and science were harder than English, but not too bad. It was as if they couldn't believe I thought school was pretty easy.   When we worked through Step 2, the teachers talked about things I never realized had anything to do with the grades I get in school, like being able to use a computer in some of my classes and having a textbook of my own to take home and use to do my work. Also, I never thought the number of students in my classes affected how I learn. I figured the more kids, the better. I was surprised about how much thought teachers put into planning what and how they teach. They take so much time to prepare. Now that we've completed Step 2, I realize how many different things affect the way I learn and how I do in school. My grades really don't provide all the information about what happens at Pioneer."

Jennifer Clayton — Pioneer High School Student

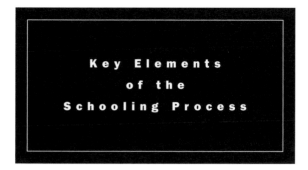

Key Elements of the Schooling Process

A number of models can be used to illustrate the schooling process, some of which are very complex. This workbook uses a simplified model containing three key elements, which are briefly described below.

Student Outcomes

What you want students to know, think, believe, value, achieve, or be able to do—the ultimate objective of schooling.

School Practices

Strategies adopted to achieve or improve your targeted student outcomes, including curriculum, instruction, assessment methods, and supporting structures.

School Inputs

Resources you have to work with, including students, staff, community support, physical plant, equipment, and budget. Since many inputs are relatively fixed, they are likely to influence the set of practices that are appropriate and the outcomes that are achievable in the short term.

School systems usually keep track of at least some student outcomes. Without collecting information on related practices and inputs, however, these schools are limited in their ability to explain changes in their outcomes. Collecting data on all three key elements—outcomes, practices, and inputs—provides a more powerful analytic tool than collecting data on only one or two elements. Although an indicator system may not enable you to prove that particular practices and inputs have a direct or causal effect on outcomes, it will allow you to monitor whether your practices and inputs are collectively having the expected impact on student outcomes, and should provide you with useful information for diagnosing why you are or are not making progress.

Pick the right mix of outcomes, practices, and inputs for assessing your performance.

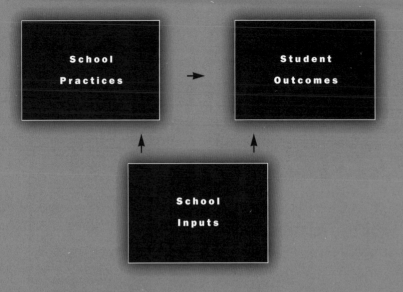

FIGURE 1 | A MODEL OF THE SCHOOLING PROCESS[7]

The above model illustrates several relationships, between 1) practices and outcomes, 2) inputs and outcomes, and 3) inputs and practices.

School practices directly affect student outcomes, or they are intended to do so. For example, in order to improve student academic achievement, your school might replace low-level academic classes with more challenging ones so that all students are exposed to rigorous coursework.

School inputs affect student outcomes by influencing the outcomes that are achievable—at least in the short term. For example, schools that enroll large numbers of economically disadvantaged students might exhibit low achievement test scores despite high-quality teaching,

because their students have low levels of initial achievement. Attaining high standards may be more of a challenge for these schools than for advantaged ones, and may require stronger improvement strategies.

School inputs also affect school practices by influencing the set of practices that are appropriate. Thus, a school with a large economically disadvantaged student population might decide to offer additional tutoring services, invest in professional development for its teachers, or completely overhaul the curriculum in order to help their students achieve the targeted outcomes.

[7] This model is adapted from Raizen and Jones (1985); Oakes (1986); Shavelson et al. (1987); Shavelson, MacDonnell, and Oakes (1989); Kaagan and Coley (1989); and Porter (1991). The *At Your Fingertips* model differs in one key way from the earlier models in that it draws a direct link between inputs and outcomes as well as an indirect link through practices.

Information on student outcomes helps answer the question:
How are our students performing?

1. Academic knowledge and cognitive skills

· Academic achievement
(for example, mathematics, reading, writing,
science, history, geography, and the arts)

· Critical-thinking/problem-solving skills

2. Social and physical development

· Self-confidence/self-esteem

· Student motivation/engagement

· Self-discipline

· Social participation/interpersonal skills

· Physical well-being and health

3. Civic competence

· Civic values/democratic beliefs

· Global perspective

· Appreciation of cultural heritage

· Appreciation of cultural diversity

4. Preparing for the world of work

· Ability to apply learning to real-world problems

· Technological literacy

· Employability/work-readiness skills

· Specific occupational competencies

· Selection/completion of a career major

· Completion of vocational program

· Attainment of industry skill certificates

5. Completing high school

· High school graduation

· Lower dropout rate

6. Success after high school

· Meet college eligibility requirements

· Placement into and success in further education
(enrollment; low rates of remediation;
passing GPA; attainment of degree, certificate,
or educational objective)

· Completion of tech-prep program

· Placement into and success in employment
(employment status and stability, wages,
advancement)

Examples of School Practices

Strategies adopted to achieve or improve your targeted student outcomes, including curriculum, instruction, assessment methods, and supporting structures.

Information on school practices helps answer the question:
What strategies are we using to improve student performance?

1. Curriculum organization
- Curriculum frameworks
- Integration across academic disciplines
- Thematic units

2. English/language arts instruction
- Writing process approach
- Whole language approach
- Phonics instruction/basal reading programs

3. Teaching diverse populations
- High expectations for all students
- Immersion/ESL/bilingual education
- Multicultural education
- Multiple intelligences approach
- Homogeneous/heterogeneous grouping

4. Instructional materials
- Textbook-based instruction
- Use of various resources and instructional tools (primary sources, calculators, manipulatives, and so on)
- Computers

5. Pedagogical approaches
- Constructivist approach/constructing meaning/active learning
- Behaviorist approach/drill and practice
- Teacher-directed instruction
- Student-centered classroom
- Whole group/small group instruction
- Cooperative learning

6. School-to-work approach
- Real-world applications
- Use of technology
- Integration of academic and vocational education
- Teaching all aspects of an industry
- Career pathways/clusters/majors
- Career academies
- Work-based learning experiences (job site visits, job shadowing, mentoring, internships, apprenticeships, service learning, and so on)
- Career guidance

7. Assessment methods
- Short-answer testing (multiple-choice, true-false, fill-ins)
- Essays
- Portfolios
- Authentic assessment (exhibitions, performance tasks, projects, laboratory assignments)
- Rubrics
- Individual grades
- Group grades

8. Supporting structures
- Block scheduling
- Common teacher planning time
- Number of course hours/periods per week assigned to teachers
- Class size
- Staff development activities
- Support for administrators and teachers
- Minimum teacher qualifications

Examples of School Inputs

Resources you have to work with, including students, staff, community support, physical plant, equipment, and budget.

Information on school inputs helps answer the question:
Who are we and what resources do we have to work with?

1. Students

· Gender and race–ethnicity

· Student and family backgrounds (economic disadvantage, language spoken in the home, parent educational attainment, and so on)

· Preexisting skills, knowledge, and abilities

· Interests and aspirations

· Student enrollment (school and class size)

2. Staff

· Student-teacher ratio

· Student-staff ratio

· Gender and race–ethnicity

· Teacher knowledge, skills, training, and experience

· Qualifications of applicants for teaching positions

3. Community support

· Community values

· Parent involvement

· School volunteers

· Business donations of funds and equipment

· Business participation on advisory boards

· Business involvement in work-based learning

4. Physical plant, equipment, and budget

· Quality and size of facilities/physical plant

· Quality and amount of equipment/technology

· School budget

· Per-pupil expenditures

5. Time available for instruction

· Length of school day

· Length of school year

STEP

Identify Related Outcomes, Practices, and Inputs

After reviewing the examples provided on the preceding pages, consider the following for your district, school, program, department, or classroom:

1. What student outcomes do you think are most important for your goals?

. . . .

. . . .

. . . .

2. What school practices do you think are most important for your goals?

. . . .

. . . .

. . . .

3. What school inputs do you think are most important for your goals?

. . . .

. . . .

. . . .

Identifying Related Outcomes, Practices, and Inputs

First, you will need to clarify the specific outcomes you are interested in monitoring and then identify the most important practices and inputs that are related to them. Although the goals you established in Step 1 described student outcomes, they may have been written in fairly broad terms. In this chapter, you will identify one or more specific outcomes for each of your goals, and then fill in the missing links of the schooling process model by identifying the practices and inputs related to those outcomes. Ultimately, you will identify specific outcomes and related practices and inputs for each of your education goals.

Identifying Specific Outcomes and Related Practices and Inputs

Based on its goal of preparing students for both further education and work, Pioneer High School identified the following specific outcomes and related practices and inputs:

School Practices

· Increase the high school's graduation requirements.

· Provide intensive after-school tutoring services.

· Offer staff development activities on applied academics and integration of academic and vocational education.

· Provide all students with meaningful work-based learning experiences, in particular, job-shadowing, mentoring, and internship opportunities.

Student Outcomes

Goal:

To prepare all students for both further education and meaningful work with advancement possibilities.

Specific Outcomes:

· Attain high academic achievement for all students, especially in English/language arts, mathematics, and science.

· Graduate from high school.

· Demonstrate work-readiness skills.

School Inputs

· School Board and parent support for increasing high school graduation requirements.

· Availability of staff and volunteers (peers, parents, workplace mentors) to provide after-school tutoring.

· Scheduled common teacher planning time.

· Employer commitment to providing work-based learning experiences.

· Student demographics affecting baseline outcomes (eligibility for free or reduced-price lunch, language spoken in the home, parent educational attainment).

STEP 2

Identify Related Outcomes, Practices, and Inputs

Worksheets

Worksheets **2.1–2.3** will help you identify the specific outcomes and related practices and inputs for the goals you established in Step 1. Although the worksheets are designed for teams, individuals can complete the activities on their own.

Since you will need to complete one set of worksheets for each goal in Worksheet 1.3, copy the duplicate worksheets at the conclusion of this workbook as many times as necessary.

2.1 — Identifying Specific Outcomes and Related Practices and Inputs

Helps you clarify the specific outcomes you are interested in monitoring and then identify the most important practices and inputs that are related to them.

2.2 — Evaluating Your Outcomes, Practices, and Inputs

Helps you evaluate the soundness of the relationships you identify in Worksheet 2.1.

2.3 — Finalizing Your Related Outcomes, Practices, and Inputs

Helps you narrow your list of related outcomes, practices, and inputs and set priorities among them.

WORKSHEET 2.1

Identifying Specific Outcomes and Related Practices and Inputs

Activities 1–5 in this worksheet help you identify specific outcomes and related practices and inputs for the goals you established in Step 1. Complete one worksheet for each goal.

1. Divide your team into small groups of three to five persons, and assign one goal from Worksheet 1.3 to each group. This will make the activity more focused and less time consuming. Depending on the number of people and goals you have, the small groups may need more than one goal to work on.

2. If you have several goals, work on them in order of their priority in Worksheet 1.3. Write down the goal you are currently working on in the space provided.

3. Discuss the specific student outcomes that are implied by your goal, and then record them in the outcomes box.

4. Working backwards, discuss the most important practices and inputs that are related to the specific outcomes you identified and record these in the appropriate boxes. What school practices will help you achieve these student outcomes? What school inputs are likely to influence the practices that are appropriate and the outcomes that are achievable in the short term?

5. Repeat activities 2–4 for each goal you were assigned, using separate worksheets.

Goal

....

....

School Practices	Student Outcomes

Be as specific as possible

Be as specific as possible

School Inputs

Be as specific as possible

Worksheet 2.2 helps you evaluate whether the relationships you identified in Worksheet 2.1 are strong enough to justify data collection, support data analysis, and lead to valid conclusions. Complete one worksheet for each goal. Discuss the following questions and note any revisions you would like to make to your set of related outcomes, practices, and inputs.

1. If you have several goals, work on them in order of their priority in Worksheet 1.3. Write down the goal you are currently working on below.

Goal ....

2. Can you be more specific in describing the student outcomes that are implied by your goal?

....

....

....

3. Are you reasonably sure that the school practices you have identified will help you improve or achieve your targeted student outcomes? Which of your identified practices are most strongly linked to your outcomes?

....

....

....

4. How confident are you that the school inputs you have identified influence either the set of practices that are appropriate or the outcomes that are achievable? Which of your identified inputs are most strongly linked to your practices and outcomes?

....

....

....

5. Which of your identified outcomes, practices, and inputs are valued or emphasized the most at your school? Which ones would key stakeholder groups be most interested in knowing something about?

....

....

....

6. Are there any outcomes, practices, or inputs that are receiving attention at your school—because they are recognized either as a problem or as a potential solution—and that should be reflected in your work on this goal?

....

....

....

Worksheet 2.3 helps you narrow your list of related outcomes, practices, and inputs to the most important ones and record them in priority order. Complete one worksheet for each goal.

1. If you have several goals, work on them in order of their priority in Worksheet 1.3. Write down the goal you are currently working on below.

Goal ....

2. Review your notes on Worksheet 2.2. Eliminate or modify any of the outcomes, practices, and inputs you identified in Worksheet 2.1. Record your final selections in priority order below.

Specific student outcomes:

1. ....
2. ....
3. ....
4. ....
5. ....
6. ....
7. ....
8. ....

Related school practices:

1. ....
2. ....
3. ....
4. ....
5. ....
6. ....
7. ....
8. ....

Related school inputs:

1. ....
2. ....
3. ....
4. ....
5. ....
6. ....
7. ....
8. ....

NEXT STEPS

Be sure to keep all completed copies of Worksheet 2.3 for each of your education goals so that you can refer to them later.

You are now ready to determine data sources and performance indicators for the priority outcomes, practices, and inputs that you have identified in this chapter.

Step 3 | Determine Data Sources and Indicators

Step 3 helps you identify data sources and develop performance indicators for the outcomes, practices, and inputs you identified as important to your education goals. The chapter emphasizes using existing data sources where possible and developing valid, reliable, and fair indicators.

"Working through Step 3 both interested and surprised me. As a counselor at Pioneer High School for the past 15 years, I thought I knew about most of the data that were maintained by the school and that everyone else was aware of these data sources, too. When I first read the chapter, I thought this would be a simple task because most of the data we needed, such as achievement test scores and transcripts, were available from the guidance office. It wasn't until our team discussed the worksheets that it became clear that not everyone was aware of the types of records kept by my office. Additionally, I began to realize there were a number of other 'data' sources that I hadn't considered. I never thought about teachers' classroom records, administrative personnel files, and funds and expenditures reports as being potential data sources. I still think that many of the 'hard data' will come out of my office—test scores, grades, and so on—but other sources of data will really round out the information we need for monitoring progress toward our goals. After brainstorming about available data sources, we really got down to brass tacks. In order to select our performance indicators, we had to decide exactly what we wanted to know. For instance, how were we going to measure teacher participation in professional development activities or the availability of school facilities? Was attendance at an in-service workshop enough, or did we want some evidence that new ideas were being applied in the classroom? Was average square footage per student a good enough indicator, or did we want some measure of the quality of facilities in addition to quantity? Could we obtain the information we wanted from existing data sources, or did we need to develop new ones? There was quite a bit of lively discussion as we weighed the possible alternatives, and everyone had good ideas to contribute."

Mr. Thomas Rountree — Head Counselor, Pioneer High School

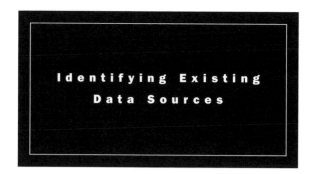
Broadly conceived, data include all of the information and records that your school routinely collects, not just numerical statistics that are maintained in a computer database. In fact, in Webster's dictionary, "data" is defined as "factual information . . . used as a basis for reasoning, discussion, or calculation."[8] Data sources can be either formal and standardized, or informal and ad hoc. Relevant data may be . . .

· *Maintained in an automated, centralized computer system at your school.* Most secondary school systems nationwide keep at least some information in an automated, centralized system. For example, a large number of school systems maintain computerized student transcripts, usually providing a record of what courses students have taken, the grades they have received, and the credits they have earned. Some electronic transcripts also include standardized achievement test scores or the number of days students have been absent from school. Moreover, some school systems maintain automated staff records, which may include professional histories (education levels and credentials), salary trends, and attendance records.

· *Maintained centrally, but kept as paper records in a filing cabinet.* Many school systems also keep centralized student records that are not automated. File folders, for instance, may contain information about students' high school plans, discipline infractions, extracurricular activities, and awards. These data may be kept in a central place such as the guidance office.

· *Decentralized, for example, maintained by individual teachers in their classrooms.* Additional information about students may be decentralized. Individual teachers often keep records about students' daily class

**Determine data sources and indicators
to measure how you are performing on your goals.**

attendance, competencies they have acquired, and performance on particular assessments. Teachers may also maintain samples of their students' work.

· *Maintained by an outside agency, such as your district office or a state or federal agency.* A last example of data sources involves information that is not necessarily kept at your school. You may find that your district office or state education agency, for instance, maintains records about your school that may be of interest to you. Sometimes, these offices issue formal performance reports—such as state report cards, vocational education performance reports, or reports on school-to-work progress measures—and sometimes they maintain the records solely for administrative purposes. Federal agencies also maintain useful data. For example, the Census Bureau publishes statistics by census tract that describe the economic and racial make-up and average educational attainment, among other characteristics of a community.

[8]*Merriam-Webster's Collegiate Dictionary,* Tenth Edition (1993), Springfield, MA: Merriam-Webster, Incorporated.

Examples of Commonly Available Data Sources

Information on students

· Enrollment records
  (enrollments, transfers, and dropouts)

· Daily attendance records

· Automated or paper student records
  (demographics, extracurricular activities)

· Automated or paper transcripts
  (course enrollments and levels, credits earned, grades)

· Standardized achievement test scores

· Occupational competency tests
  (e.g., VOCATs)

· Work-readiness assessments
  (e.g., WorkKeys)

· Locally developed pre- and post-tests

· Exit exams
  (for a program, grade, or entire school)

· Guidance records
  (career plans, participation in guidance activities)

· Disciplinary action records
  (referrals, infractions, detentions, suspensions)

· Employer evaluations
  (e.g., of cooperative education students)

· Student follow-up surveys
  (employment and wage rates, further education and training)

· College entrance exam scores
  (and the proportion of students taking the test)

· Postsecondary enrollment records
  (enrollment in further education)

· Postsecondary transcript data
  (grades, remedial coursework, continuation in tech-prep programs)

Information on teachers or administrators

· Personnel files
  (teacher training and certification, staff development activities, salary trends, staff evaluations, continuing education credits)

· Attendance records

· In-service records

School-level information

· Community surveys or needs assessments

· Funds and expenditures
  (per-pupil expenditure trends)

· Reports prepared for or by the district or state

· Agreements with postsecondary institutions or businesses and industry groups

· Records kept about school meetings, parent-staff conferences, school visits

· Records on tutorial programs
  (students, teachers, tutors)

· Dropout and completion rates

· Student-faculty ratios

· Numbers and types of diplomas awarded

· Information collected for purposes of applying or responding to grantors

· Previous reports on or evaluations of classrooms, programs, or the entire school

Developing New Data Sources

You may find that the data currently available do not shed light on some of the outcomes, practices, and inputs you identified in Step 2. If important pieces of information are missing, you may need to collect additional data. Because developing new data sources can be costly in terms of money and time, you will want to limit them to sources that provide crucial information that is not available from existing ones.

The table below offers some examples of targeted new data sources you may want to develop. If you choose to pursue one of these special data collections, you will need to think further about the specific information you hope to gain from the effort.

Appendix D contains a list of resources you may want to consult when developing new data collection instruments such as those listed below.

Examples of Targeted New Data Sources

- Surveys and questionnaires (of teachers, students, parents, employers, community members)

- Interviews or focus groups (with the same groups as above)

- Teacher logs/diaries

- Classroom observations (of actual instructional practices and student responses)

- Alternative assessments (e.g., work samples, portfolios, senior projects, and performance tasks)

- Locally developed pre- and post-tests

STEP 3

Determine Data Sources and Indicators

Related to the goals you are pursuing ...

· What relevant information do you personally collect, see, or use in a typical day?

....

....

....

· What relevant information do you know of that is collected by other teachers, departments, programs, or offices at your site? By an outside office or agency?

....

....

....

· What kinds of relevant information are used to support decisions, actions, and changes at your site?

....

....

....

· What do you already know about your school's performance on these goals? Where did you get your information? What existing data sources could be tapped to inform your goals?

....

....

....

· What new sources of information might be helpful?

....

....

....

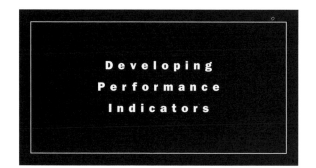

Developing Performance Indicators

Performance indicators are statistics that help measure progress on your outcomes, practices, and inputs. Indicators are usually expressed as

· Counts,

· Averages,

· Percents, or

· Rates.

While data sources act as a record or repository of raw information, performance indicators transform that information into a relevant measurement.

Outcome indicators are of vital importance, because student performance is ultimately where you want to see results. However, indicators can also be developed for practices and inputs in order to monitor important factors affecting outcomes. For example: Are key practices being implemented? Are key inputs changing in either positive or negative ways? Practice and input indicators help paint a more complete picture of system performance than do outcome indicators alone. Monitoring practice and input indicators can also help suggest possible strategies to improve student outcomes.

Determine Data Sources and Indicators

Determining Data Sources and Indicators

Based on its goal of preparing all students for both further education and work, Pioneer High School identified the following priority data sources and corresponding indicators for its outcomes, practices, and inputs.

Targeted Outcomes		
Specific Student Outcomes	**Priority Data Sources**	**Corresponding Performance Indicators**
· Attain high academic achievement for all students, especially in English/language arts, mathematics, and science	· Achievement test scores · Student transcripts	· Average reading, mathematics, and science gains on state tests · Percent of graduating seniors meeting the state university's entrance requirements
· High school graduation	· Guidance records	· High school graduation rate
· Demonstrate work-readiness skills	· Employer evaluations	· Percent of seniors participating in work-based learning experiences who received a satisfactory or higher rating

Targeted Practices

Related School Practices	Priority Data Sources	Corresponding Performance Indicators
· Increase the high school's graduation requirements	· Program of Studies	· Minimum number of credits in core academic subject areas required for graduation
· Provide intensive after-school tutoring services	· Tutor sign-in sheets	· Number of students participating at least 1) once a semester and 2) once a week
· Offer staff development activities on applied academics and integration of academic and vocational education	· Staff development records	· Number of teachers attending in-services on integration of academic and vocational education
	· Teacher survey	· Percent of participating teachers reporting they have collaborated with other teachers to develop integrated lesson plans
· Provide all students with meaningful work-based learning experiences (in particular, job shadowing, mentoring, and internship opportunities)	· School-to-work liaison records	· Percent of graduating seniors who participated in an organized work-based learning experience

Targeted Inputs

Related School Inputs	Priority Data Sources	Corresponding Performance Indicators
· Availability of staff and volunteers (peers, parents, workplace mentors) to provide after-school tutoring	· Guidance records	· Number of tutoring hours logged by staff and volunteers
· Scheduled common teacher planning time	· Master schedule	· Number of minutes per week of scheduled common teacher planning time
· Employer commitment to providing work-based learning experiences	· School-to-work liaison records	· Number of work-based learning openings for 1) job shadowing, 2) mentoring, and 3) internships
· Student demographics affecting baseline outcomes	· Guidance records	· Percent of students 1) eligible for free or reduced-price lunches, 2) who speak a language other than English at home, and 3) whose parent(s) completed high school

Using Qualitative Information

Because they are expressed as statistics, performance indicators are essentially quantitative. As such, they offer several advantages, including comprehensiveness, succinctness, precision, and comparability. Additionally, quantitative indicators are particularly useful for summarizing large amounts of information.

On the other hand, qualitative information—describing what people actually say, do, think, or feel—puts a human face on quantitative data. It provides depth and detail and may increase a person's understanding of a situation, but often lacks generalizability.

HOW MIGHT YOU USE QUALITATIVE INFORMATION AS PART OF YOUR PERFORMANCE INDICATOR SYSTEM?

· *Transform qualitative information into quantitative indicators.* It is sometimes possible to quantify quali-

tative information—for example, the number of teachers who use small group instruction at least once a week, or the percent of students who demonstrate classroom engagement. Doing so generally requires 1) defining or standardizing key terms and concepts and 2) collecting representative data. What do you mean by "small group instruction" and "classroom engagement"? By "a regular basis"? What should count as instances of these phenomena? After defining key terms, you will then need to gather information from a representative group. You might attempt to survey all teachers or observe all second-period classrooms, or you might select a random subset of these groups for data gathering. Appendix D contains a list of resources for designing and implementing surveys, interviews, observations, and other qualitative data collection methods.

· *Illustrate quantitative data with qualitative information.* Make your quantitative indicators come alive by gathering descriptive examples to illustrate important data. Qualitative information is particularly useful when explaining your performance indicator data to nontechnical audiences.

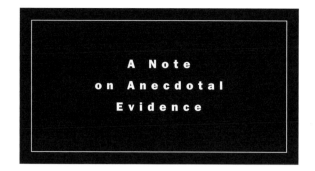

Anecdotal evidence—spontaneous comments or casual observations—is one type of qualitative information. Teachers and administrators often rely on anecdotal evidence to make decisions (Cooley 1983). For example, a student mentions after class that the day's activity was her favorite. A parent calls to voice concern over a homework assignment. A teacher expresses enthusiasm about a recent in-service workshop. In some cases, anecdotal evidence may be transformed into performance indicators, but many times such evidence is used by individual teachers or administrators on an ad hoc basis. It is possible, however, to improve the quality of this evidence and subsequently to improve its power.

Anecdotal evidence is compelling, because it concerns real people in real time. Typically, it is more vivid and personal than other, more formal types of data. The main problem with anecdotal evidence, though, is that it may be totally unrepresentative. The one person who comes forward to express his views may hold an entirely different opinion from the silent majority. Although basing a decision on a single comment or observation

can be misguided and counterproductive, ignoring such evidence can waste an important source of information.

WHAT MIGHT YOU DO ABOUT ANECDOTAL EVIDENCE?

· *Start by asking one more person her opinion or making one more observation.* As long as you have the time and believe the information to be important, continue gathering evidence, one person or observation at a time. Remember, any additional information you gather will improve the reliability of your data.

· *Decide what your relevant "survey universe" is.* If you could, would you speak to all students in your fourth-period class, or students in all of your classes? Would you speak to the parents of students of a particular teacher or the parents of all students in the school? Would you talk to the teachers who attended the recent in-service or to all teachers?

· *Sample randomly from this universe.* If possible, decide randomly which person to speak to next or what class to observe next. You can pick names out of a hat, or let your pencil fall blindly on a roster. It is natural to want to speak to someone who is easy to talk to, easy to reach, or provides thoughtful comments. However, what makes this person stand out in your mind may also differentiate the person from the general group. You are more likely to obtain representative information by being deliberately random in your investigations.

STEP

3

Determine Data Sources and Indicators

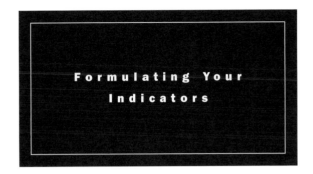

Formulating Your Indicators

There are several important considerations when formulating your performance indicators, including the following:

· **The numerical form each indicator will take.**

· **Details of who, what, and when to measure.**

· **Whether to measure attainment or gains.**

· **What comparisons to make among subpopulations.**

Making decisions about these issues early on will help you build a solid foundation for collecting and analyzing your performance indicator data. The first three issues directly affect the formulation of the performance indicators themselves—that is, how they are worded and what they measure. Consequently, they determine what data you will collect. Deciding to make comparisons among different groups of students also has a profound impact on data collection and recordkeeping, since it necessitates not only gathering results but also keeping track of these results and related characteristics for individual students. By addressing the four issues noted above thoughtfully, it will be easier for you to develop a quality indicator system. Vaguely conceived indicators, in contrast, will be subject to various misinterpretations and may make data collection and analysis exceedingly difficult. Because you are building a performance indicator system that may be in place for several years, it is important to be as clear and precise as possible in formulating your indicators from the outset.

Considering Numerical Form

You will need to decide how each performance indicator should be expressed. As mentioned earlier, indicators usually take the form of counts, averages, percents, or rates. The following example illustrates variations on a theme:

· Number of students completing high-level mathematics courses.

· Average number of credits students earned in high-level mathematics courses.

· Percent of students completing high-level mathematics courses.

· Rate of completion of high-level mathematics courses.

When deciding on the appropriate form, you should consider what specific information each form provides. While one form may be more valuable in a particular situation, a combination of forms may be best in another.

Indicators often raise additional questions. For example, *counts* may raise questions about context. If you learned that 188 students completed high-level mathematics courses, you might be interested to know what share of the total student population this number represents. Similarly, *averages* are good summary statistics, but they may obscure interesting variations. Although it may be useful to know that students earned an average of 1.0

credits in high-level mathematics courses, you might wonder how these credits were distributed. Did most students take one high-level course, or was there a small group of students earning 2.0 to 3.0 high-level credits, while most students earned zero credits? To investigate, you might want to know the *percent* of students earning different numbers of credits. Finally, you might also want to know at what *rate* students who initially enrolled in these courses ultimately completed them. Generally, a single indicator cannot answer all questions, so you will need to decide what information is most important to you, and then select the number and types of indicators that satisfy your information needs.

Considering Who, What, and When to Measure

Developing quality performance indicators requires that you be precise. In order to avoid confusion over the meaning of an indicator—and threaten the usefulness and credibility of your performance data—it is important to address the following questions for each indicator before beginning to collect your data:

· *Who is your relevant population?* For each indicator, you will need to decide what group makes up the relevant population—for example, all students in your school or students in a particular grade. The relevant population acts as the denominator when calculating indicators that take the form of percents, averages, or rates. For example, you may be interested in looking at the percent of juniors and seniors who have completed high-level mathematics courses, since underclassmen are less likely to enroll in these courses.

· *What condition(s) must be met in order to be counted in the statistic?* In order to be counted in a performance indicator, students who are members of your relevant population must satisfy one or more specific conditions. For example, juniors or seniors must complete a high-level mathematics course. Furthermore, completion may be defined as receiving a grade of D- or better, and high-level mathematics courses may be defined as including Algebra 2, Trigonometry, and Calculus. Generally, the more precise you can be in describing important details of your indicators, the better.

· *When must the condition be met?* It also helps to clarify what the relevant period of time is during which the above condition(s) must be met. For example, you might be interested in investigating the total number of students in your school who completed high-level mathematics courses in a given year. This one-year time frame provides an indication of the annual level of participation in high-level mathematics courses. Alternatively, you might be interested in investigating the percent of seniors who completed at least one high-level mathematics course during their high school careers. This four-year time frame provides an indication of how well seniors might be prepared to pursue postsecondary education. Answering the "when" question also has implications for data storage, since the longer the interval during which important conditions can be met, the more extensive are the records that must be kept.

The three key questions—who, what, and when—are interconnected. Making decisions about one often helps clarify another.

STEP

Considering Whether to Measure Attainment or Gains

Another consideration in developing your performance indicators is whether to measure attainment at a single point in time or gains achieved by the same persons over time. With respect to student outcomes, measuring attainment focuses on whether students have achieved a specified level of skill, knowledge, or ability, while measuring gains focuses on whether students have improved over time. The following examples illustrate this difference:

· Percent distribution of the highest mathematics courses completed by seniors (measures attainment).

· Percent of students not passing mathematics at mid-year who have successfully completed the course at the end of the year (measures gains).

· Average difference in mathematics test scores between fall and spring for 11th graders (measures gains).

Measuring only attainment provides only partial information about performance at your school and can lead to false conclusions and poor decisions. For example, measuring only attainment may miss the fact that low performers have made large gains despite not yet attaining performance targets. Deciding to withdraw support for strategies that achieved these gains might be premature. Selecting a mix of attainment and gain indicators, on the other hand, helps to capture the full spectrum of performance at your school and provides you with more complete information on which to base decisions.

Monitoring trends over time in performance indicator data is discussed in Step 6.

Considering What Comparisons to Make Among Subpopulations

Finally, you will want to consider what comparisons are important to make among different groups of students. Performance indicators that summarize results for an entire population—that is, for all students in the school or in a particular grade—are important and useful. They not only provide a snapshot of overall performance but also can signal areas that require general attention. However, summary statistics can hide important differences in how groups are performing. In order to target improvement efforts effectively, it is usually wise to compare performance on your indicators for selected subgroups. For example, you might compare performance based on different demographic characteristics or different educational experiences:

· Gender

· Race–ethnicity

· Language proficiency

· Socioeconomic background

· Grade levels

· Classrooms

· Course levels (basic, regular, advanced)

· Participation in career academies, career majors, occupational training, and so on.

Identifying differential performance might lead you to develop different improvement strategies than you might have developed based on summary statistics alone.

Select one of the outcomes, practices, or inputs you identified in Step 2, and then consider the following questions:

· What indicator(s) could you develop to measure that outcome, practice, or input?

....

....

· What numerical forms could the indicator(s) take?

....

....

· Who is your relevant population (the denominator for calculating your indicator[s])?

....

....

· What condition must be met in order to be counted in the indicator(s), and when must it be met?

....

....

· Should you measure attainment or gains—or both—and how would you do so?

....

....

· What subpopulations do you want to compare on the indicator(s)?

....

....

STEP

Determine Data Sources and Indicators

Ensuring the Quality of Your Indicators

After selecting your initial set of performance indicators, it is important to step back and examine them with a critical eye. Performance indicators should

· **Be valid.**

· **Be reliable.**

· **Be fair.**

· **Avoid creating unintended incentives.**

If your indicators are not valid, reliable, or fair, you may make unsound judgments and act in ways that are inappropriate or even detrimental to your education goals. Additionally, indicators can sometimes create unintended incentives. For instance, tracking grade point average can create a subtle pressure on teachers to inflate grades. In extreme cases, particular indicators can even adversely affect education and learning. For instance, overemphasis on standardized achievement test scores can deflect teaching and learning away from valued skills not assessed by the test.

Particularly when your school attaches strong positive or negative consequences to indicator performance, you will need to ensure that your indicators satisfy the criteria listed above.

Ensuring Validity

Validity reflects the extent to which a performance indicator actually measures the underlying phenomenon of interest. If you want students to develop critical thinking skills, for example, then student achievement test scores would be a valid indicator, if the test that was used specifically assessed these skills. If the test emphasized memorization and recall, on the other hand, it would be an invalid measure of critical thinking skills.

Validity also refers to how appropriately indicator data are used. An indicator may be valid for some uses and not for others. For example, in the case of student achievement tests, it might be valid for guidance counselors to use test scores to help place students; for teachers to diagnose their students' strengths and weaknesses based on these scores and focus classroom instruction on weak areas; or for principals to identify low-scoring classrooms and encourage teachers to develop strategies to raise performance in these classrooms. However, it might not be a valid use of student achievement test scores for school districts to base merit pay bonuses for teachers on these scores, since test scores gathered from a single point in time measure cumulative learning, rather than the unique contribution of individual teachers to student achievement.

IN ORDER TO ENSURE THAT YOUR PERFORMANCE INDICATORS ARE VALID, YOU CAN TAKE THE FOLLOWING STEPS:

· Consider how well an indicator reflects the outcome, practice, or input it is intended to describe. Identify and implement better and more valid indicators where possible.

· Think ahead to the kinds of decisions you may make based on an indicator. Assess how well the indicator supports these decisions.

Ensuring Reliability

Reliability reflects the consistency with which an indicator produces the same results on different occasions or in different circumstances. In the case of standardized tests, reliability also reflects the consistency of different forms of the same test. If an indicator is reliable, it provides reasonably accurate results.

Indicators that lack reliability do not produce meaningful results and cannot support sound comparisons across groups or over time. For example, your school may decide to require student portfolios to assess critical thinking skills, which are to be graded on a three-point scale: 1) basic, 2) proficient, and 3) exemplary. Without receiving sufficient guidelines or training about how to apply this rating scale, however, teachers may apply it in different ways. Thus, the designation "exemplary" may mean very different things to different teachers, and students who attain this rating may exhibit widely varying skills. Consequently, an indicator such as "the percent of students attaining an 'exemplary' rating on the new portfolio assessment" will be practically meaningless. Unless the criteria for an "exemplary" rating are defined clearly and attention is paid to assessing the consistency with which teachers apply the rating, this indicator may provide misleading information. Alternative assessments and performance indicators that promise greater validity than traditional ones must achieve a degree of reliability in order to live up to this promise.

IN ORDER TO ENSURE THAT YOUR PERFORMANCE INDICATORS ARE RELIABLE, YOU CAN TAKE THE FOLLOWING STEPS:

· For your different indicators, investigate how consistently and accurately data are reported or collected.

· Consider establishing standard definitions or data collection practices. For example, consider forming a task force of teachers to develop a rubric for grading student portfolios and to train other teachers in its use.

Ensuring Fairness

Fairness reflects the extent to which an indicator is free of bias. If an indicator is fair, it treats all subgroups and populations similarly with respect to the key factors being assessed. An indicator is unfair—or biased—if students perform differently for reasons that are irrelevant to the purpose of the indicator. For example, a reading test that included a story set on a golf course might include items that were more accessible to some students than others, in which case the fairness of the test could be called into question. Unfair and biased indicators can result in incorrect interpretations of group performance and misdirected improvement strategies.

IN ORDER TO ENSURE THAT YOUR PERFORMANCE INDICATORS ARE FAIR, YOU CAN TAKE THE FOLLOWING STEPS:

· Identify factors that might disadvantage or benefit particular groups of students on an indicator.

· Eliminate or modify any indicators where irrelevant factors are likely to affect performance.

· Involve stakeholders with different perspectives to participate in designing, reviewing, and implementing your indicator system.

Avoiding Creation of Unintended Incentives

The purpose of a performance indicator system is to provide information that supports school improvement efforts. If you use indicators to identify strengths and weaknesses, develop appropriate improvement strategies, and successfully implement those strategies, then performance on your selected indicators should improve. However, pressure to perform well on the indicators can create incentives to improve the indicator data themselves, without improving underlying performance. These actions tend to distort the meaning of indicator data.

All efforts to improve indicator data directly should not be viewed as "cheating." Stakeholders can be expected to take all reasonable steps to improve indicator performance. However, once these "improvements" have been made and initial gains on the indicators have been achieved, you are then faced with improving underlying performance, if you hope to continue to demonstrate improvement.

Distorting influences can erode confidence in your performance indicators, and consequently in your improvement efforts. To help avoid this problem, you can take the following steps:

· Try to implement indicators whose "meaning is resistant to erosion by reasonable, accepted, and ethical actions that might be taken" to improve performance (Haertel 1986).

· Keep track of and report all actions taken that significantly affect performance on the indicators, particularly when sharp increases or decreases in performance occur.

· Consider eliminating any performance indicators that are particularly susceptible to distortion. If there are good reasons not to eliminate these indicators, then take steps to guard against possible distortions.

· Attempt to match stakes or consequences to indicator quality.

Worksheets

Worksheets 3.1–3.5 will help you identify data sources and develop performance indicators for the outcomes, practices, and inputs you identified in Step 2. Although the worksheets are designed for teams, individuals can complete the activities on their own. Since you will need to complete one set of worksheets for each of your education goals, copy the worksheets at the back of the workbook as many times as necessary.

First, obtain copies of completed Worksheet 2.3 for each of your education goals. This worksheet contains the related outcomes, practices, and inputs for the goals you established in Step 1. If you are working as part of an improvement team, divide into small groups of three to five people, with each group selecting one or more goals. Designate a group spokesperson who will share

your results with the rest of the improvement team and a recorder who will create a final worksheet to give to the meeting facilitator for the project files.

3.1 — Identifying Data Sources

Helps you identify existing and new data sources for your outcomes, practices, and inputs.

3.2 — Developing Performance Indicators

Helps you develop performance indicators corresponding to each of your data sources.

3.3 — Refining Your Indicators

Helps you develop the most appropriate formulations of your performance indicators.

3.4 — Developing a Final List of Indicators

Helps you assess the quality of your performance indicators and develop a final list of indicators for each outcome, practice, and input.

3.5 — Developing a Data Collection Plan for Your Indicators

Helps you develop a plan for collecting data on your final list of performance indicators.

Activities 1–6 in this worksheet help you identify existing and new data sources for the outcomes, practices, and inputs you identified in Worksheet 2.3. You are provided with three copies of the worksheet: "A" for outcomes, "B" for practices, and "C" for inputs. Depending on the number of outcomes, practices, and inputs you identified in Worksheet 2.3, you may need to make additional copies of these worksheets.

1. Write the goal you are working on at the top of the worksheet.

2. Transfer your outcomes from Worksheet 2.3 to the left-hand column of Worksheet 3.1A in order of priority.

3. Discuss with your group or consider on your own where data might be found for each outcome. Write these data sources in the middle column of Worksheet 3.1A. Be expansive. Be creative. Allow yourself to come up with anything that will provide you with the information you believe will be helpful. You will weed out less important data sources as you continue to develop your indicators.

4. It may be that existing data sources do not provide useful information about the outcomes you have identified. If this is so, space has also been provided in the right-hand column to indicate any crucial new data sources you may need.

5. Repeat activities 1–4 for your practices and inputs, using Worksheets 3.1B and 3.1C, respectively.

6. After completing the worksheet, groups should report the results of their work to the rest of the improvement team.

GOAL:

Outcomes From Worksheet 2.3	Existing Data Sources	Crucial New Data Sources
PRIORITY # _____		
PRIORITY # _____		
PRIORITY # _____		

GOAL:

Practices From Worksheet 2.3	Existing Data Sources	Crucial New Data Sources
PRIORITY #_____		
PRIORITY #_____		
PRIORITY #_____		

GOAL:

Inputs From Worksheet 2.3	Existing Data Sources	Crucial New Data Sources
PRIORITY # _____		
PRIORITY # _____		
PRIORITY # _____		

Activities 1–5 in this worksheet help you develop performance indicators for each data source you identified in Worksheet 3.1. You are provided with three copies of the worksheet: "A" for outcomes, "B" for practices, and "C" for inputs. Depending on the number of outcomes, practices, and inputs you have identified, you may need to make additional copies of these worksheets.

1. Write the goal you are working on at the top of the worksheet.

2. Transfer your outcomes from Worksheet 3.1A to the appropriate boxes in order of priority.

3. For each outcome, think about what you really want to know. Review the different data sources you identified in Worksheet 3.1A. Which data sources will provide you with the most important and relevant information? List the most important ones in order of priority on Worksheet 3.2A.

4. For each data source, think about what information can be produced concerning the associated outcome. Brainstorm with your group or on your own about possible performance indicators that can be derived from the data source and write them in the corresponding boxes. Remember to write your indicators in terms of counts, percents, averages, and rates, and to be as specific as possible. You may identify more than one indicator for each data source.

5. Repeat activities 1–4 for your practices and inputs, using Worksheets 3.2B and 3.2C, respectively.

GOAL:

OUTCOME # _____ : ....

Priority Data Sources | **Corresponding Performance Indicators**

OUTCOME # _____ : ....

Priority Data Sources | **Corresponding Performance Indicators**

OUTCOME # _____ : ....

Priority Data Sources | **Corresponding Performance Indicators**

GOAL:

PRACTICE #_____: ....

Priority Data Sources	Corresponding Performance Indicators
....	....
....	....
....	....
....	....
....	....
....	....

PRACTICE #_____: ....

Priority Data Sources	Corresponding Performance Indicators
....	....
....	....
....	....
....	....
....	....
....	....

PRACTICE #_____: ....

Priority Data Sources	Corresponding Performance Indicators
....	....
....	....
....	....
....	....
....	....
....	....

GOAL:

INPUT #_____: ....

Priority Data Sources

Corresponding Performance Indicators

INPUT #_____: ....

Priority Data Sources

Corresponding Performance Indicators

INPUT #_____: ....

Priority Data Sources

Corresponding Performance Indicators

Activities 1–4 in this worksheet help you refine the performance indicators you identified in Worksheet 3.2. You are provided with three copies of the worksheet: "A" for outcomes, "B" for practices, and "C" for inputs. You may need to make additional copies of these worksheets.

1. Write the goal you are working on at the top of the worksheet.

2. Transfer your outcomes from Worksheet 3.2A to the appropriate boxes in order of priority.

3. For each outcome, review the performance indicators you identified in Worksheet 3.2A and answer the questions listed below. Revise your indicators as needed and record the revised indicators in order of priority in the space provided. You might also find it useful to identify subpopulations whose performance on the indicators you think is important to examine. Repeat this activity for each outcome.

· Indicators can be expressed as counts, averages, percents, and rates. Each form provides different information. Have you selected the most valuable *numerical forms* for your indicators?

· Who are your *relevant populations* (the denominators for calculating your indicators)? Should the indicators be rewritten to clarify who the relevant populations are?

· What *condition(s)* must be met—and when—in order to be counted in each statistic? Should the indicators be rewritten to clarify these conditions?

· Should you measure *attainment or gains*—or both? Do you need to modify your indicators to do so?

· What *subpopulations* might you want to compare for each indicator based on demographic characteristics or educational experiences?

4. Repeat activities 1–3 for your practices and inputs, using Worksheets 3.3B and 3.3C, respectively.

GOAL:

OUTCOME #_____: ....

Indicator #1 ....

Indicator #2 ....

Indicator #3 ....

Indicator #4 ....

Indicator #5 ....

Subgroup comparisons ....

....

OUTCOME #_____: ....

Indicator #1 ....

Indicator #2 ....

Indicator #3 ....

Indicator #4 ....

Indicator #5 ....

Subgroup comparisons ....

....

OUTCOME #_____: ....

Indicator #1 ....

Indicator #2 ....

Indicator #3 ....

Indicator #4 ....

Indicator #5 ....

Subgroup comparisons ....

....

GOAL:

PRACTICE #_____: ....

Indicator #1 ....

Indicator #2 ....

Indicator #3 ....

Indicator #4 ....

Indicator #5 ....

Subgroup comparisons ....

....

PRACTICE #_____: ....

Indicator #1 ....

Indicator #2 ....

Indicator #3 ....

Indicator #4 ....

Indicator #5 ....

Subgroup comparisons ....

....

PRACTICE #_____: ....

Indicator #1 ....

Indicator #2 ....

Indicator #3 ....

Indicator #4 ....

Indicator #5 ....

Subgroup comparisons ....

....

GOAL:

INPUT #_____: ....

Indicator #1 ....

Indicator #2 ....

Indicator #3 ....

Indicator #4 ....

Indicator #5 ....

Subgroup comparisons ....

....

INPUT #_____: ....

Indicator #1 ....

Indicator #2 ....

Indicator #3 ....

Indicator #4 ....

Indicator #5 ....

Subgroup comparisons ....

....

INPUT #_____: ....

Indicator #1 ....

Indicator #2 ....

Indicator #3 ....

Indicator #4 ....

Indicator #5 ....

Subgroup comparisons ....

....

Activities 1–6 in this worksheet help you assess the quality of your performance indicators and develop a final list of indicators for each outcome, practice, and input. You are provided with three copies of the worksheet: "A" for outcomes, "B" for practices, and "C" for inputs. You may need to make additional copies of these worksheets.

1. Write the goal you are working on at the top of the worksheet.

2. Transfer your outcomes from Worksheet 3.3A to the appropriate boxes in order of priority.

3. For each outcome, review the performance indicators you identified in Worksheet 3.3A and answer the questions listed below. Revise your indicators as needed and record the revised indicators in order of priority in the space provided. Space is also provided to record any thoughts you may have about important subpopulation comparisons, steps to improve accuracy and consistency, actions or decisions to avoid, and steps to guard against distorting the data. Repeat this activity for each outcome.

· How well do the indicators reflect the outcome they are intended to describe? Are there other ways to measure the outcome that provide more valid information?

· What kinds of actions or decisions do you think might be based on the results of these performance indicators? Do you think the quality of the data will support these actions or decisions? What actions or decisions should be avoided so that you do not misuse the data?

· How consistently and accurately are data currently being reported or collected on these indicators? What definitions or data collection practices could be standardized to make the data more reliable?

· Do you think there are any irrelevant factors that might significantly disadvantage or benefit particular groups of students on the indicators? Should any indicators be eliminated or modified in light of this potential bias?

· Are there any indicators that seem particularly susceptible to distortion? What steps might be taken to avoid creating unintended incentives?

4. Repeat activities 1–3 for your practices and inputs, using Worksheets 3.4B and 3.4C, respectively.

5. After completing the worksheet, groups should report the results of their work to the rest of the improvement team.

6. Give one copy of the completed worksheet to your meeting facilitator for the project files.

GOAL:

OUTCOME #_____: ....

Indicator #1 ....

Indicator #2 ....

Indicator #3 ....

Indicator #4 ....

Indicator #5 ....

Notes ....

....

OUTCOME #_____: ....

Indicator #1 ....

Indicator #2 ....

Indicator #3 ....

Indicator #4 ....

Indicator #5 ....

Notes ....

....

OUTCOME #_____: ....

Indicator #1 ....

Indicator #2 ....

Indicator #3 ....

Indicator #4 ....

Indicator #5 ....

Notes ....

....

GOAL:

PRACTICE #_____: ....

Indicator #1 ....

Indicator #2 ....

Indicator #3 ....

Indicator #4 ....

Indicator #5 ....

Notes ....

....

PRACTICE #_____: ....

Indicator #1 ....

Indicator #2 ....

Indicator #3 ....

Indicator #4 ....

Indicator #5 ....

Notes ....

....

PRACTICE #_____: ....

Indicator #1 ....

Indicator #2 ....

Indicator #3 ....

Indicator #4 ....

Indicator #5 ....

Notes ....

....

GOAL:

INPUT #_____: ....

Indicator #1 ....

Indicator #2 ....

Indicator #3 ....

Indicator #4 ....

Indicator #5 ....

Notes ....

....

INPUT #_____: ....

Indicator #1 ....

Indicator #2 ....

Indicator #3 ....

Indicator #4 ....

Indicator #5 ....

Notes ....

....

INPUT #_____: ....

Indicator #1 ....

Indicator #2 ....

Indicator #3 ....

Indicator #4 ....

Indicator #5 ....

Notes ....

....

Activities 1–8 in this worksheet help you develop a plan for collecting data on your final list of performance indicators. You are provided with three copies of the worksheet: "A" for outcomes, "B" for practices, and "C" for inputs. You may need to make additional copies of these worksheets.

1. Write the goal you are working on at the top of the worksheet.

2. Transfer your outcome indicators from Worksheet 3.4A to the first column of Worksheet 3.5A.

3. Refer back to Worksheet 3.2A to determine the data sources for your indicators. Not all of your indicators may be reflected on Worksheet 3.2A, since you may have added indicators in subsequent steps. For new indicators, think about where you will obtain the relevant data. Record all data sources and locations for your final indicators in the second column of Worksheet 3.5A.

4. Discuss and record what next steps need to be taken to obtain the indicator data.

5. Discuss and record who will assume primary responsibility for the next steps.

6. Decide on a target date for each next step.

7. Repeat steps 1–6 for your practice and input indicators, using Worksheets 3.5B and 3.5C, respectively.

8. Give one copy of the completed worksheet to your meeting facilitator for the project files.

GOAL:

Outcome Indicators from Worksheet 3.4A	Data Source/Location from Worksheet 3.2A	Next Steps	Person Responsible	Target Date

WORKSHEET 3.5B · Developing a Data Collection Plan for Practice Indicators

GOAL:

Practice Indicators from Worksheet 3.4B	Data Source/Location from Worksheet 3.2B	Next Steps	Person Responsible	Target Date

GOAL:

Input Indicators from Worksheet 3.4C	Data Source/Location from Worksheet 3.2C	Next Steps	Person Responsible	Target Date

NEXT STEPS

For future reference, be sure to collect completed copies of
Worksheets 3.4 and 3.5 for each of your education goals.

You are now ready to gather your indicator data.
Once you have gathered them, proceed to Step 4.

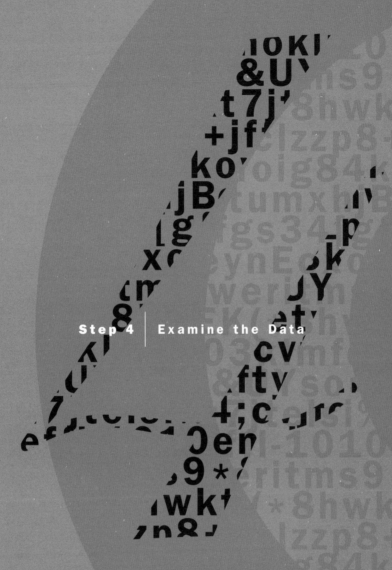

Step 4 | Examine the Data

In Step 4, you will use the data you have assembled to determine how you are currently performing on your education goals. The first year of data collection allows you to create a baseline against which to compare future progress. This section introduces several techniques for examining and interpreting your data and offers alternate ways of presenting your findings.

"I am a fairly new teacher here at Pioneer High School and this performance indicator project is the first long-term group project I have engaged in as a teacher. I'm still learning how I can improve my own teaching and how I can better prepare my students for their futures. I was pretty quiet during the goal-setting process and some of the earlier steps. I just didn't feel like I knew enough about the school and the surrounding community to be setting goals. However, as it turned out, the goals we developed were not very different from those I would have set for Pioneer High School myself —or any school for that matter. As I became more comfortable on the team, I contributed more and became more vocal. When we got to Step 4, I felt that I was definitely in my element. Being able to share my own mathematics skills and knowledge with my peers and colleagues boosted my self-confidence, and I know that my contributions during the workshop were important to the team as a whole. Certainly, they could have learned how to interpret and present the data without me, but they really appreciated my assistance. When you honor each person's gifts and skills, the whole group benefits."

Alicia Martinez — Mathematics Teacher, Pioneer High School

Compiling Your Data

This chapter assumes that after developing performance indicators in Step 3, you have taken some time to assemble your data. Not all of the data you need or desire may be available, however. You may still be developing some new data sources, or the timing of Step 4 may be such that certain data cannot be obtained until later in the year.

Some of your data may be in raw form: a list of different types of disciplinary offenses and their frequency, for example, or photocopies of student transcripts. You may need to do some work to transform these raw data into their corresponding performance indicators—for instance, the total number of disciplinary offenses, the rate of offenses per number of students enrolled, the percent of seniors who took Algebra 1 or higher during their high school careers, and the percent of juniors and seniors taking a mathematics course during the current academic year.

If you want help in turning your raw data into indicator statistics, you may want to contact your school or district's management information system and evaluation departments, or your registrar and guidance offices. If such assistance is not available, you may want to consult with someone who has experience with compiling and analyzing data, such as one of your mathematics or science teachers, a professor at a local college, or a businessperson with experience in data analysis. An expert can help you tally statistics, interpret results, and present your findings clearly.

Examine your data to enrich your understanding of your performance.

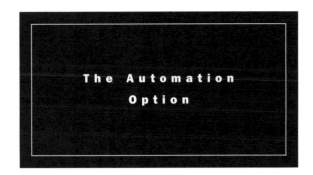

This chapter discusses several methods of data analysis that can help you examine your performance indicator data. While it is helpful to understand the analytical concepts, it is not necessary in this day and age to compute the statistics manually. Therefore, it is a good idea for you to consider using a computer to compile, analyze, and present your data.

A basic computer with software that is capable of recording, sorting, and summarizing information (including a spreadsheet program for calculating and analyzing basic statistics, a word processing program for writing summary reports, and a graphics program for displaying your findings) will be adequate for most of your data analysis needs. The size of your student body and the comprehensiveness of your data analysis efforts will dictate what kind of computer you need. Most computer stores have experts who can help you decide what computer or software packages to buy and how to set up the necessary programs.

Before purchasing a computer or software package, it is important to understand clearly what equipment, software, and training the vendor can provide. If possible, ask a computer specialist from your school system or a statistics professor from a nearby university, or recruit someone from a local firm that does data analysis to assist you when purchasing a product. Educate the expert about what kind of work you expect to do on the computer and what kind of computer experience you have. Another option is to call other schools who have already automated performance information. If you do so, ask these schools what companies have provided them with good service and what computer programs they find most helpful.

Examining Your Data

Although you may not "crunch the numbers" yourself, you will be examining your school's performance data. You will also be responsible for helping convey their meaning to others. Step 4 describes the following process for examining, interpreting, and summarizing your data:

- Develop a first impression.

- Examine the spread, or distribution, of your data.

- Translate the data into concrete terms.

- Examine differences among important subgroups.

- Examine the relationships among outcome, practice, and input data.

- Present your data effectively.

Before explaining this process in detail, an example from Pioneer High School on the next few pages illustrates how it works.

STEP

Examine the Data

Mrs. Martinez, a mathematics teacher on the Pioneer High School improvement team, was assigned to gather and examine attendance data. She obtained an attendance report from the central office indicating that Pioneer's average daily attendance (ADA) rate was 92 percent. At first blush, Mrs. Martinez was pleased, since 92 on a scale of 100 generally corresponds to an "A" grade. However, upon further analysis, she realized that 92 percent ADA meant that Pioneer students missed, on average, almost three weeks of school during the year (based on a 180-day school year). She considered this to be unacceptable performance.

By translating ADA into concrete terms—the number of days missed—Mrs. Martinez identified attendance as a possible area needing improvement. Next, she wanted to know what factors affected student attendance. To answer this question, she investigated which students were chronically absent and when they were missing school. As Mrs. Martinez exam-ined attendance patterns by gender, grade level, and day of the week, one finding stood out:

Average Daily Attendance by Day of the Week	
Day of the week	Rate
Monday	95%
Tuesday	97%
Wednesday	94%
Thursday	92%
Friday	82%

By disaggregating attendance data by day of the week, Mrs. Martinez learned that student attendance peaked on Tuesday and declined steadily thereafter. Additionally, students were less likely to attend school on Friday than on any other day. Mrs. Martinez believed this pattern was particularly troublesome because most teachers tested their students on Fridays.

Mrs. Martinez presented her findings to the rest of the Pioneer High School improvement team. In her presentation, she included the following graph illustrating her key finding:

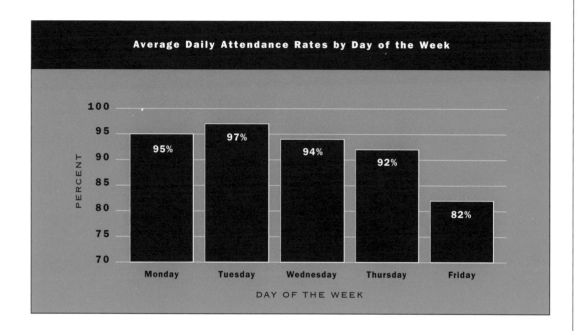

She asked her fellow team members to review the data and speculate about the meaning of the results. The team reviewed her report, discussed their interpretations of the data, and raised some additional questions. As a result of the discussion, the team decided to make attendance a priority. To do this, they recommended three actions: creating a friendly competition by reporting student and staff attendance over the loudspeaker as part of daily announcements; moving the weekly pep rally from Wednesday to Friday afternoon; and sending a

bulletin to all teachers to inform them of the attendance situation and to suggest that they test students during the first part of the week.

The example above illustrates how you might use data to learn about your school's performance on your indicators and generate discussion about possible causes and solutions. However, you might draw different conclusions from the evidence that Mrs. Martinez uncovered.

After reviewing the Pioneer High School example, consider the following questions:

- What might explain Pioneer High School's attendance pattern?

....

....

....

....

....

....

- What additional information—if any—would you like to have before drawing conclusions?

....

....

....

....

....

- What would you do to improve attendance at Pioneer High School?

....

....

....

....

....

**Developing a
First Impression**

As discussed in Step 3, performance indicators typically take the form of counts, averages, percents, and rates. These simple statistics summarize your data using a single number and provide an overall picture of your school's performance in a specific area, as shown in the example below.

Sample Performance Indicators and Results	
Performance indicator	**Performance results**
· Number of graduating seniors completing high-level mathematics courses during high school	188
· Average number of credits earned by graduating seniors in high-level mathematics courses during high school	1.0
· Percent of graduating seniors completing high-level mathematics courses during high school	61%
· Rate of completion of high-level mathematics courses during high school (rate at which students who enrolled in such courses completed them)	75%

When reviewing your performance on your selected indicators, you will begin by developing a first impression. Do your performance results seem high or low, or do they match your expectations? How well do you seem to be performing in this area? If you have similar data for another school in your district or for the entire state, you may want to compare your initial results against these data to help form an initial impression of your performance.

Examine the Data

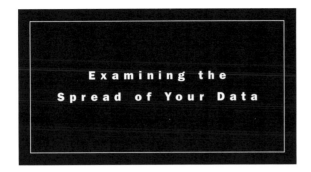

Examining the Spread of Your Data

While single statistics provide information about overall performance in an area, examining the spread, or distribution, of your data helps you define the character of your school's performance, pinpoint strengths and weaknesses, and develop appropriate improvement strategies.

Using a single statistic to represent a large set of data is useful because people are more likely to remember one number and can easily compare it to other meaningful values. However, a single statistic does not tell the complete story. The table below describes the mathematics course-taking patterns of students in greater detail than does the statement "61 percent of graduating seniors completed high-level mathematics courses during high school." Specifically, the distribution reveals that 31 percent of seniors completed Algebra 2, 21 percent completed "other advanced" courses, and 9 percent completed Calculus as their highest mathematics course.

By providing a description of the spread of your data along with single summary statistics, you convey more of the story and develop a more accurate picture of your performance. Additionally, such analysis allows you to target specific areas or groups of students needing attention.

Percent of Graduating Seniors by Highest Mathematics Course Completed in High School	
Highest mathematics course completed	**Percent of seniors completing the course**
· Less than Prealgebra	8%
· Prealgebra	6%
· Algebra 1	11%
· Geometry	14%
· Algebra 2	31%
· Other advanced mathematics*	21%
· Calculus	9%

* Includes Algebra 3, Trigonometry, Analytic Geometry, Precalculus, and Probability and Statistics.

SOURCE: U.S. Department of Education, National Center for Education Statistics (1995), *Vocational Education in the United States: The Early 1990s,* Table 49.

Measures of Spread

Three common methods used to describe the spread, or distribution, of data are as follows:

- *Listing the range of the data.* When indicating the range of the data, you report the lowest and highest values, usually along with the average (or mean). This helps determine how spread out performance is on an indicator and helps you identify unacceptably high or low values. In the previous example, for instance, you might find it is unacceptable that 14 percent of seniors completed Prealgebra or lower as their highest mathematics course and decide to work toward having all students complete at least Algebra 1 or higher.

- *Identifying outliers.* Outliers are extreme high or low values that have a tendency to distort averages or means. Outlying performers may have particular needs that require focused attention. Sometimes, removing outliers from your data analysis will yield more policy-relevant results.

- *Separating the data into quartiles or deciles.* The range indicates the "high" and "low," but does not provide information about whether your data are distributed evenly, bunched around the middle, or concentrated at one or both ends. Quartiles divide the data into four equal parts: the bottom 25 percent, lower middle 25 percent, upper middle 25 percent, and top 25 percent of values, and deciles divide the data into 10 equal parts. Depending on the situation, you might decide to focus improvement strategies on one or more quartiles or deciles. Subdividing the data in this manner can raise questions about the evenness of school practices and lead you to investigate underlying causes and possibly change strategies.

Graphing the distribution of your data helps you understand and interpret these measures of spread.

These are only three techniques that can be used to describe data spread. Information about other techniques, such as standard deviation and variance (and about calculating the mean and other descriptive statistics), can be found in any basic statistics textbook.

STEP

Examine the Data

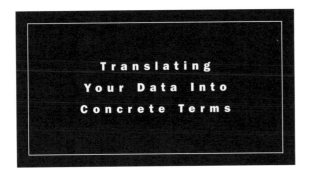

Translating Your Data Into Concrete Terms

It usually helps to translate your performance indicator statistics into concrete terms that all stakeholders can understand. As seen in the ADA example earlier in the chapter, statistics can be misleading. For instance, an ADA of 92 percent might at first glance look high, but realizing that this translates into an average of 14 days of school missed each year puts a different cast on the data. In the mathematics course-taking example, describing the distribution by type of course taken gives you more information than a single summary statistic. When possible, it helps to translate your averages, percents, and rates into concrete terms, such as the number of persons, days, classes, courses, and so on that are affected, in order to facilitate interpretation.

Examining Differences Among Important Subgroups

Performance indicators that summarize results for an entire population—for all students or classrooms in the school, for example—are important and useful. They provide a snapshot of overall performance and can signal areas that require general attention. However, summary statistics can hide important differences in how student groups are performing and how practices are being implemented. In order to focus improvement efforts effectively, it is usually wise to compare performance on your indicators for selected subgroups. In Step 3, you thought about what comparisons you might make on your different indicators in order to collect supporting data. In this step, you will compare important subgroups based on the demographic characteristics and educational experiences you identified as important.

Examining differences in performance among subgroups involves the following:

- **Observing the sign or direction of a difference or trend in the data.**

- **Evaluating the size of a difference or strength of a trend.**

- **Testing the statistical significance of a difference or trend for sample data.**

- **Determining the practical importance of a difference or trend.**

Evaluating trends in performance over time will be discussed further in Step 6.

Observing the Sign or Direction of a Difference or Trend

The sign or direction of a difference indicates whether a group of students are performing better or worse than another, whether a practice is more or less prevalent than another, or whether there is a discernible upward or downward tendency in the data. For example, the following table indicates that, on average, teachers are more likely to use "writing across the curriculum" strategies than they are to use "integrating academic and vocational education" strategies (26 versus 17 percent of classes). The data also indicate that the general tendency to use writing across the curriculum strategies *decreases* as the grade level of a class increases. In contrast, the tendency for teachers to integrate academic and vocational education *increases* with grade level.

Percent of Classes in Which Teachers Reported Using Various Instructional Strategies at Least Once a Week					
Instructional strategy:	9th-grade	10th-grade	11th-grade	12th-grade	Total
Writing across the curriculum (various practices)	34	30	22	18	26
Integrating academic and vocational education (various practices)	15	16	18	19	17

Based on your initial examination of the data, you might want to 1) investigate why teachers are less likely to use writing across the curriculum strategies and more likely to integrate academic and vocational education in higher grades; 2) develop ways to increase the use of writing across the curriculum strategies in higher grades; and 3) develop ways to increase the use of integrating academic and vocational education strategies in all grades, especially the lower ones.

Evaluating the Size of a Difference or Strength of a Trend

The following questions are important to ask before allocating resources to specific improvement efforts:

· How large is the disparity in group performance or in the prevalence of different practices?

· How strong is an upward or downward tendency in the data?

· Is a difference large enough or a trend steep enough to warrant increased attention?

In the previous example, you might decide that the disparity in using integration strategies between the 9th and 12th grades (15 versus 19 percent of classes) is not large enough for you to focus on the differential use of this instructional strategy across grade levels. Instead, you might focus on the relatively low incidence of implementing integration strategies in general. In contrast, you might decide that the steep decline in using writing across the curriculum warrants some attention.

Testing the Statistical Significance of a Difference or Trend for Sample Data

Noting the magnitude of a difference provides a quick, rough estimation of its importance. When analyzing sample data—specifically, randomly sampled data—it is also necessary to test a difference statistically to see whether it is "significant."[9]

Most of the data you will use in this workbook will probably describe an entire population, such as all students or teachers in the school. Even when some data are missing (for instance, only 75 percent of teachers respond to a survey about instructional practices), they are said to describe the intended population. In some instances, however, you may work with sample data. Some standardized tests, for example, may be administered only to a random sample of students. Or, you may decide to collect new data from only a random sample of respondents in order to save time and money. In those cases, you will need to pay attention to the statistical significance of any perceived differences or trends. Significance testing takes into consideration not only the size of a difference but also the size of the populations being compared and how their performance varies. In other words, significance testing contributes another piece of evidence about whether a perceived difference is important and warrants attention. Large apparent differences in sample data may not be statistically significant—that is, may not be statistically different from zero at an accepted error level.

Determining the Practical Importance of a Difference or Trend

Ultimately, you must use your judgment about whether a difference or trend in the data has any practical importance. For example, suppose the average standardized test scores for girls and boys were 280 and 300, respectively. A statistical test might determine that this difference was "significant." However, the 20-point difference might mean that boys, on average, answered only two more questions correctly than girls. You might conclude that this was not an important practical difference in group performance. Instead, you might decide that the fact that your school scored 100 points below the state average was a more important difference and, therefore, warrants looking at the overall performance of the school on the test.

Weighing sign, size, and significance, as well as evaluating the practical importance of any differences in performance, can help you focus on what is important and allow you to tailor your improvement efforts appropriately.

[9] Statistical significance refers to whether a difference between two groups is statistically discernible at a specified error level, usually a 5 percent error (or significance) level. Further discussion about conducting statistical significance tests can be found in any basic statistics book under confidence intervals and hypothesis testing.

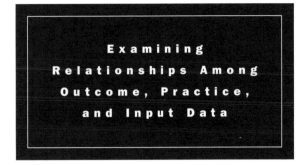

Examining Relationships Among Outcome, Practice, and Input Data

· Two indicators tend to move in the same direction (positive correlation).

· Two indicators tend to move in opposite directions (negative correlation).

· An indicator appears to be unaffected by the movement of another (no correlation).

Once you have gathered your baseline data, you can examine the key relationships you identified in Step 2 in order to confirm your hypotheses about related outcomes, practices, and inputs. For example: Are standardized mathematics test scores indeed related to the number of mathematics credits that students earned? Is the use of hands-on activities associated with greater student engagement?

There are three general types of relationships among data:

You may find it useful to test your assumptions about relationships among related outcomes, practices, and inputs by graphing data for key pairs of indicators. A clear upward or downward trend in the data would support your assumptions.[10]

Interpreting changes over time is discussed in Step 6.

[10] In addition to graphing your data, a common statistical technique that can be used to determine the direction and strength of a linear relationship between two variables is the correlation coefficient (used with ordered variables containing increasing or decreasing categories). Information on calculating correlation coefficients and other relevant statistical tests can be found in any basic statistics book.

Relationship Between Mathematics Credits Earned and Test Scores	
Number of mathematics credits earned in high school	**Average mathematics test score in senior year**
2.0	252
2.5	250
3.0	278
4.0	287

A Warning About Drawing Causal Inferences

You should be careful to remember that correlation does not imply causation. Just because two indicators are related does not mean that one causes the other. In fact, a variety of additional factors may be at work behind the scenes.

For example, although the number of mathematics credits earned in high school may be positively correlated with 12th-grade mathematics test scores, the operative factor may be the types of mathematics courses taken rather than the number. Because the types of mathematics courses taken may be somewhat correlated with the number of courses taken, there may appear to be a causal relationship between the number of credits earned and test scores. A better indicator of relevant practices may be the highest level of mathematics course taken in high school, with peak test performance associated with, for instance, Algebra 2 (depending on the content covered by the test). When examining relationships among outcome, practice, and input data, it is always good to be on the lookout for better and more relevant indicators.

Examine the Data

**Presenting
Your Data Effectively**

There are two main reasons to be concerned about how you present your data:

· Clarity of analysis.

· Clarity of communication.

First, it is easier to examine and understand your data if they are presented clearly. Second, since you will most likely share your data with others, it may help to highlight key findings with tables and graphs. Your audience may not have the background and experience that you have gained after working through the first three steps in this workbook. When sharing information, it is helpful to make it as clear and easy to understand as possible.

This section provides you with examples of ways to present your data and guides you in creating effective tables and graphs. Of course, the section provides only introductory material. Hundreds of books have been written on presenting data effectively, and you may want to consult one of these sources. However, this section is designed to help you get started.

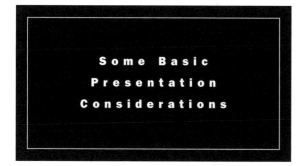

When examining tables and graphs, your audience needs to know precisely what they are looking at. You can assist them by making sure that the following items are clearly noted in the title, labels within the table or figure, or a footnote:

- *Who or what is represented.* Your audience needs to know precisely who or what is represented in a table or figure. For example: Does the table represent all students in the school? All classrooms? Or just a subset of these? Using "10th graders" may be more precise than "students," or "mathematics classrooms" more precise than "classrooms." Be as specific as possible in your descriptions.

- *Unit of measurement used.* What may seem obvious to you may not be so obvious to your audience. It is important to indicate the unit(s) of measurement used in a table or graph. For example: Does the table describe the *percent* of classrooms containing computers? The annual number of *dollars* allocated to purchasing computer equipment? The total *number* of computers in the school? It is better to err on the side of stating the obvious than to leave your audience guessing.

- *Size of the denominator.* It is important to provide the number of people or other entities (classrooms, courses, and so on) that form the base—or denominator—of the statistic(s) presented in a table or graph. If 30 percent of mathematics classrooms use calculators on a regular basis, your audience may want to know the total number of mathematics classrooms included in the survey. If the average standardized achievement test score in mathematics for 10th graders was 269 (on a scale of 500), your audience may want to know the total number of 10th graders who took the test. Describing the denominator helps explain the context for your statistics.

- *Time period covered.* Your data may cover different time periods for different indicators. For example, student enrollment counts may be tallied on a specific date in the fall, while standardized achievement tests may be administered in the spring and only every other year. Depending on the timing of your data analysis or presentation, you may be examining data from different semesters or school years. In order to avoid confusion, it is helpful to include in your table or figure the time frame covered by the data. Doing so can also help avoid confusion when looking at trend data in the future.

- *Data source.* A note on your data source(s), typically included at the bottom of a table or figure, helps your audience understand the nature of the data (whether it is primarily objective or subjective, for example) and make an initial judgment about the data's reliability and validity. For instance, you might evaluate findings about the number of teachers integrating academic and vocational education differently, if the data are self-reported or based on classroom observations by other teachers. Describing the data source can help stakeholders focus on developing additional ones for crucial performance areas.

Clearly presenting the above information helps your audience quickly answer its initial questions about "what are these data" and "where did they come from," so they can proceed to the more important questions about "what do the data mean" and "what are we going to do about it"?

Tables Versus Figures

Americans live in a very visual society; our eyes are drawn to graphical representations and tend to glaze over when presented with a table filled with numbers. However, this preference is not reason enough to always use a graph to present your data. You may, for instance, want to display a wider range of information using tables when early in the interpretation phase, and then highlight key findings using graphs or figures. The type of visual presentation you choose should be based on your purpose: do you want to provide a wide range of information and allow readers to determine what is important and to draw their own conclusions? Do you want to highlight specific differences between identified groups? Should particular trends be emphasized? The answers to these questions have implications for how you choose to display your data.

On the next page are two different ways in which you can present the same information.

Tables

Often tables can be more effective than graphs in presenting information. If you have a lot of information that you want to convey in a limited amount of space, then you should use a table. While graphs can be very effective in drawing attention to your findings, they can be confusing if they contain too much information. When creating tables, highlight statistics and comparisons that you find interesting either by using bold print or by putting bullet points underneath the table that highlight your most interesting findings.

Figures

A number of different kinds of figures are presented on the following pages, along with some general guidelines about how to construct and use them. They are followed by space where you can record your thoughts regarding the attractiveness and clarity of the figures. Later on when your improvement team discusses how to disseminate the results of your data collection, you can refer back to these notes.

Alternative Presentations

In the examples below, vocational teachers were asked how much they emphasize academic concepts in their teaching.

How Much Do Vocational Teachers Emphasize Academic Concepts in Their Teaching?			
	1993 (percent)	1995 (percent)	1997 (percent)
Quite a lot	22	27	31
Some	33	36	46
Very little	44	27	23
Don't know	0	9	0
Number of teachers responding	9	11	13

NOTE: In each year, all teachers in the school were given a questionnaire about instructional practices. In this table, vocational teacher responses are reported separately.

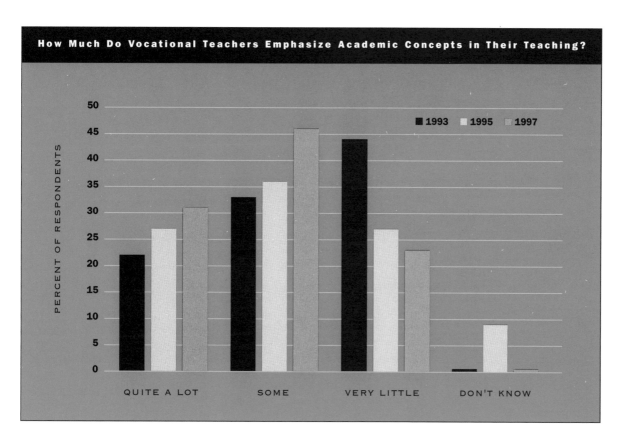

How Much Do Vocational Teachers Emphasize Academic Concepts in Their Teaching?

NOTE: In each year, all teachers in the school were given a questionnaire about instructional practices. In this figure, vocational teacher responses are reported separately.

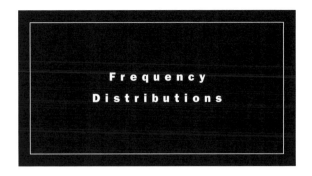

Frequency Distributions

A frequency distribution shows how many times relevant values have occurred—in other words, it displays the "frequency" of each value. A basic frequency distribution plots the relevant values on the horizontal axis and the number of occurrences on the vertical axis. In the example below, the graph displays the frequency distribution of grades awarded in a typical public high school.

By graphing your data in this manner you can discern how they are distributed. Are they spread evenly, clustered at one or both ends of the distribution, or distributed normally?[11] Frequency distributions can also help you identify outliers, locate average (mean and median) values, and visually separate your data into quartiles or deciles. Descriptions of additional data presentation methods, such as stem-and-leaf displays and box and whisker plots, can be found in many basic statistics textbooks or books on exploratory data analysis.

[11]A normal distribution is a bell curve that conforms to specific mathematical properties.

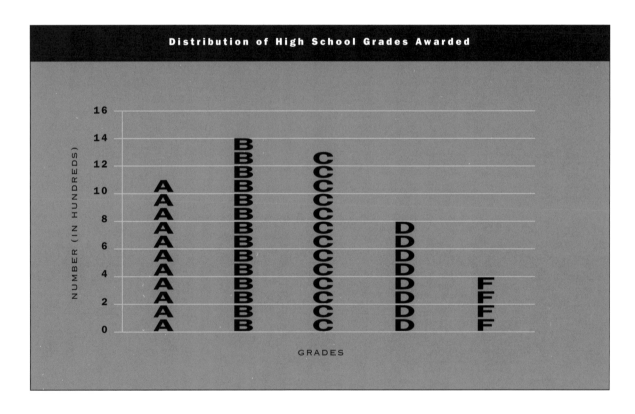

Distribution of High School Grades Awarded

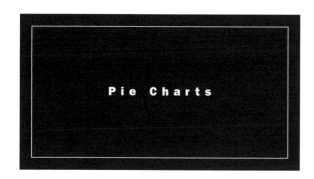

Pie Charts

The pie chart might be the most simple, yet arresting, graphical presentation. It is best used to illustrate parts of a whole relationship, where percents sum to 100. If you wish to call attention to a particular category, you can design your chart so that the pie piece "explodes" from the remainder of the pie.

The chart below illustrates the table on page 120.

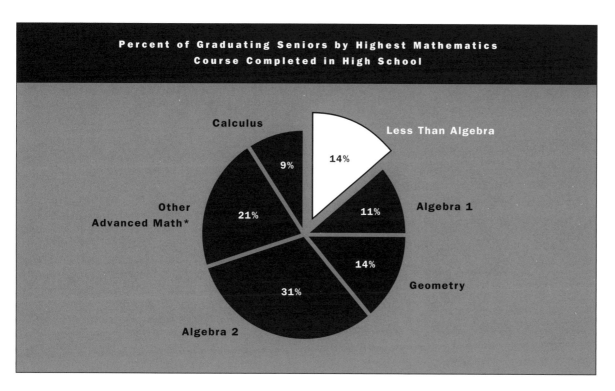

Percent of Graduating Seniors by Highest Mathematics Course Completed in High School

* Includes Algebra 3, Trigonometry, Analytic Geometry, Precalculus, and Probability and Statistics.

SOURCE: U.S. Department of Education, National Center for Education Statistics (1995), *Vocational Education in the United States: The Early 1990s,* Table 49.

Examine the Data

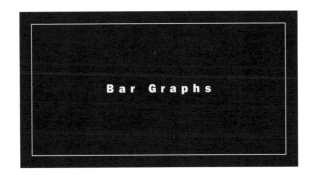

Bar Graphs

Bar graphs are useful for making visual comparisons, especially where there is a strong trend in the data or if differences among two or three groups are striking. They are frequently used because they are simple to read and understand. However, you should limit the amount of information that you include in bar graphs, since additions can make these simple figures quite busy. The more information that you display, the harder it may be for your audience to interpret the graph.

The graph below illustrates the table on page 124.

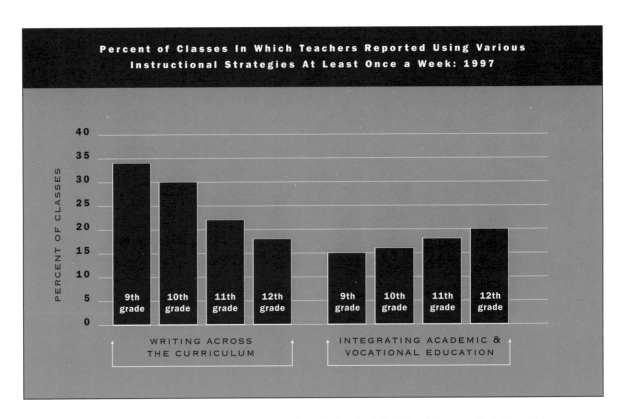

NOTE: In spring 1997, teachers in the school were given a questionnaire about instructional practices in their different classrooms. About 75 percent of the teachers responded.

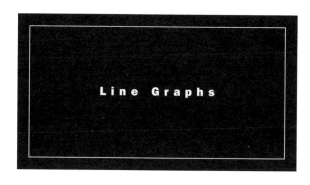

Line Graphs

Line graphs are particularly useful when looking at information collected over a number of years, and help you track trends. Be sure to select a scale that fills up the visual space.

This graph depicts national trends in the dropout rate.

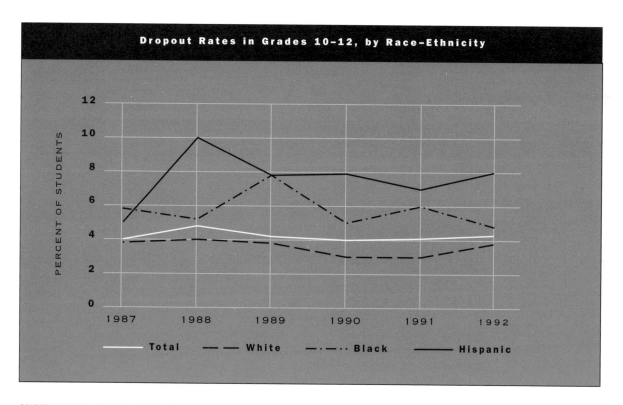

Dropout Rates in Grades 10–12, by Race–Ethnicity

SOURCE: M. McMillen, P. Kaufman, E. Germain Hausken, and D. Bradby (1993), *Dropout Rates in the United States: 1992* (NCES 93-464) (Washington, DC: U.S. Department of Education, National Center for Education Statistics).

Scatterplots

A scatterplot graphs the relationship between two variables—such as two performance indicators. One indicator is plotted on the horizontal axis and the other on the vertical axis. Pairs of data are located as dots on the graph. After graphing all pairs of data, you can draw a line through the data points to indicate the general trend in the data. Alternatively, you can use a computer spreadsheet program to calculate and plot the "regression line." Scatterplots help you determine whether key pairs of indicators move in the same or opposite directions or appear to be unaffected by each other. They can also be used to predict performance on one indicator, when performance on the other is known.

The following scatterplot illustrates the table on page 126. Individual pairs of data were plotted, rather than only the averages listed in the table.

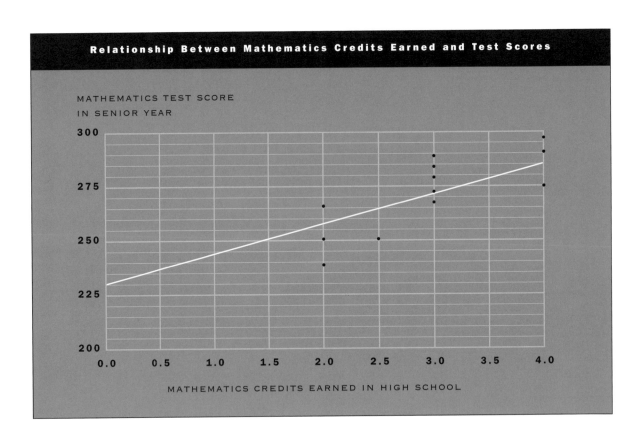

Relationship Between Mathematics Credits Earned and Test Scores

MATHEMATICS TEST SCORE IN SENIOR YEAR

MATHEMATICS CREDITS EARNED IN HIGH SCHOOL

· What are your impressions of the different graphs?

....

....

....

....

....

....

....

· What kinds of information do they convey well?

....

....

....

....

....

....

....

· Which of your performance data would be best presented by the different graphs?

....

....

....

....

....

....

Worksheets 4.1–4.2 will help you examine and summarize your performance data and identify additional information needs. Although the worksheets are written to accommodate teams, individuals can complete the activities on their own.

First, obtain copies of completed Worksheets 3.4A–C for each of your education goals. These worksheets contain your final lists of indicators for the outcomes, practices, and inputs related to your goals. If you are working as part of an improvement team, divide into small groups of three to five people, with each group selecting one or more goals.

4.1 — Examining Your Data

Worksheets 4.1A–C help you examine and interpret your outcome, practice, and input data. Since you will need to complete one worksheet for each of your indicators, copy the duplicate worksheets at the back of the workbook as many times as necessary.

4.2 — Summarizing Your Findings

Helps you summarize your findings for each goal.

Copy the goal, outcome, and indicator you are currently working on from Worksheet 3.4A, and then discuss the questions under 1–5 below and record your responses in the spaces provided.

Goal ....

Outcome #_____: ....

Indicator #_____: ....

1. Getting to Know Your Data

What is the data source for this indicator? ....

What is the unit of measurement? ....

Who or what is included in the statistic? ....

What is the size of the denominator (if applicable)? ....

What is the time period covered? ....

What additional information do you need to understand the data you are working with? ....

....

2. Your First Impressions

Does your performance on the indicator in question seem high? Low? Does it match your expectations? How? ....

....

....

Translate the data into concrete terms (the number of persons, days, classes, courses, and so on, that are affected): ....

....

Does this information contribute anything to your understanding of the data? If so, what? ....

....

....

3. Examining the Spread, or Distribution, of Your Data

You may want to graph or otherwise examine the distribution of your data.

What is the average (mean) of the data? ....

What do you think should be an acceptable average (mean)? Why? ....

....

3. Examining the Spread, or Distribution, of Your Data—continued

What is the range of your data? Highest value _____ Lowest value _____

What do you think should be an acceptable range? Why? ....

....

Are there any outliers (extreme high or low values that are distorting the mean)? If so, what are they?

....

Do you think your outlying performers have particular needs that should be addressed? If so, what might they be?

....

Divide your data either into *quartiles* (highest 25 percent, upper middle 25 percent, lower middle 25 percent, lowest 25 percent) or *deciles* (10 equal parts).

Which groups, if any, exhibit exemplary performance? Satisfactory performance? Unsatisfactory performance?

....

4. Subgroup Comparisons

Referring back to Worksheets 3.3A and 3.4A, what subgroup comparisons did you conclude were important to make on this indicator (based on different student demographics or educational experiences)?

....

Are any student groups performing better or worse than the others? If so, what patterns emerge? ....

....

What is the magnitude of these differences or trends? Are they practically important? ....

....

If the data are based on a random sample rather than an entire population, are the perceived differences statistically significant?

....

5. Interpreting Your Data

How do you think your school is performing on the indicator in question? ....

....

....

What do the distribution of your data and your subgroup comparisons suggest about how improvement efforts should be focused?

....

....

What additional information do you need to understand or interpret these data? ....

....

Copy the goal, practice, and indicator you are currently working on from Worksheet 3.4B, and then discuss the questions under 1–5 below and record your responses in the spaces provided.

Goal ....

Practice #_____: ....

Indicator #_____: ....

1. Getting to Know Your Data

What is the data source for this indicator? ....

What is the unit of measurement? ....

Who or what is included in the statistic? ....

What is the size of the denominator (if applicable)? ....

What is the time period covered? ....

What additional information do you need to understand the data you are working with? ....

....

2. Your First Impressions

Does your performance on the indicator in question seem high? Low? Does it match your expectations? How?

....

....

Translate the data into concrete terms (the number of persons, days, classes, courses, and so on, that are affected):

....

Does this information contribute anything to your understanding of the data? If so, what? ....

....

....

3. Examining the Spread, or Distribution, of Your Data

You may want to graph or otherwise examine the distribution of your data.

What is the average (mean) of the data? ....

What do you think should be an acceptable average (mean)? Why? ....

....

3. Examining the Spread, or Distribution, of Your Data—continued

What is the range of your data? Highest value _____ Lowest value _____

What do you think should be an acceptable range? Why? ....

....

Are there any outliers (extreme high or low values that are distorting the mean)? If so, what are they?

....

Do you think your outlying performers have particular needs that should be addressed? If so, what might they be?

....

Divide your data either into *quartiles* (highest 25 percent, upper middle 25 percent, lower middle 25 percent, lowest 25 percent) or *deciles* (10 equal parts).

Which groups, if any, exhibit exemplary performance? Satisfactory performance? Unsatisfactory performance?

....

4. Subgroup Comparisons

Referring back to Worksheets 3.3B and 3.4B, what subgroup comparisons did you conclude were important to make on this indicator (based on different teacher or classroom characteristics, for example)? ....

....

Are any practices more (or less) prevalent in particular circumstances than others? If so, what patterns emerge?

....

What is the magnitude of these differences or trends? Are they practically important? ....

....

If the data are based on a random sample rather than an entire population, are the perceived differences statistically significant?

....

5. Interpreting Your Data

How do you think your school is performing on the indicator in question? ....

....

....

How do these practice data contribute to your understanding of your related outcome data? ....

....

....

What additional information do you need to understand or interpret these data? ....

....

Copy the goal, input, and indicator you are currently working on from Worksheet 3.4C, and then discuss the questions under 1–5 below and record your responses in the spaces provided.

Goal ....

Input #_____: ....

Indicator #_____: ....

1. Getting to Know Your Data

What is the data source for this indicator? ....

What is the unit of measurement? ....

Who or what is included in the statistic? ....

What is the size of the denominator (if applicable)? ....

What is the time period covered? ....

What additional information do you need to understand the data you are working with? ....

....

2. Your First Impressions

Does your performance on the indicator in question seem high? Low? Does it match your expectations? How?

....

....

Translate the data into concrete terms (the number of persons, days, classes, courses, and so on, that are affected):

....

Does this information contribute anything to your understanding of the data? If so, what? ....

....

....

3. Examining the Spread, or Distribution, of Your Data

You may want to graph or otherwise examine the distribution of your data.

What is the average (mean) of the data? ....

If applicable, what do you think should be an acceptable average (mean)? Why? ....

....

3. Examining the Spread, or Distribution, of Your Data—continued

What is the range of your data? Highest value _____ Lowest value _____

If applicable, what do you think should be an acceptable range? Why? ....

Are there any outliers (extreme high or low values that are distorting the mean)? If so, what are they? ....

....

Do you think the outlying data require particular attention? If so, what might this be? ....

....

Divide your data either into *quartiles* (highest 25 percent, upper middle 25 percent, lower middle 25 percent, lowest 25 percent) or *deciles* (10 equal parts).

How widely dispersed are the data? Does this raise any concerns? If so, what are they? ....

....

4. Subgroup Comparisons

Referring back to Worksheets 3.3C and 3.4C, what subgroup comparisons did you conclude were important to make on this indicator (based on different buildings, departments, or programs in your school, for example)?

....

Are there important differences in inputs in different circumstances? If so, what patterns emerge? ....

....

What is the magnitude of these differences or trends? Are they practically important? ....

....

If the data are based on a random sample rather than an entire population, are the perceived differences statistically significant?

....

5. Interpreting Your Data

How do you think your school is performing on the indicator in question? ....

....

....

How do these input data contribute to your understanding of your related outcome data? ....

....

....

What additional information do you need to understand or interpret these data? ....

....

Write down the goal you are working on below. After examining all of your indicator data on the outcomes, practices, and inputs related to this goal, it is time to summarize your findings. Review all copies of Worksheets 4.1A–4.1C for this goal, and then discuss the questions under 1–4 below. Record your responses in the spaces provided.

Goal ....

1. Deciding on the Implications of Your Indicator Data

How do you think your school is performing on this goal? ....

....

....

What evidence do you have to support this opinion? ....

....

Why do you think you are performing at the current level? Cite specific evidence, where possible.

....

....

What additional information do you need to understand your performance on this goal? ....

....

2. Examining Relationships Among Your Outcome, Practice, and Input Data

Refer back to Worksheet 2.3 to review the outcomes, practices, and inputs you decided were related to this goal.

Are there any relationships between pairs of specific outcomes, practices, and inputs that might help you better understand your performance on this goal? If so, what are they? ....

....

....

Graph or examine the relationship between the relevant indicators for key pairs of outcomes, practices, and inputs. Do the data appear to move in the same direction, in opposite directions, or do they appear to be unaffected by one another?

....

....

How does examining these relationships contribute to your understanding of your performance on this goal? Remember, correlation does not imply causation. ....

....

....

3. Presenting Your Findings

To prepare for presenting your findings to the entire improvement team (or additional audiences), decide what are the most important points you would like to make about how your school is performing on this education goal. . . . .

. . . .

. . . .

. . . .

. . . .

How would you illustrate each of these points? Your choices include single statistics, tables, and graphs (frequency distributions, pie charts, bar graphs, line graphs, and scatterplots).

. . . .

. . . .

. . . .

. . . .

Who will be responsible for:

· Preparing the presentation materials . . . .

· Making the presentation . . . .

· Additional research . . . .

4. Improving Your Indicator Data

What performance indicators related to this goal would you eliminate in the future? . . . .

. . . .

. . . .

What performance indicators would you add to help better understand your performance on this goal? . . . .

. . . .

. . . .

What existing data sources need to be improved? How? . . . .

. . . .

. . . .

What new data sources need to be developed? . . . .

. . . .

. . . .

Be sure to keep completed copies of Worksheet 4.2 for each of your education goals so that you can refer to them in the future.

You are now ready to set performance targets for your indicators.

Step 5 | Set Performance Targets

Step 5 will help you set performance targets—the levels of performance you will strive for on your indicators. Setting targets involves assessing your current performance, specifying desired levels of performance, and then devising strategies to achieve them. Performance targets are specific and measurable. They bring the school improvement process full circle, back to the original goals you established in Step 1. If your goals were not measurable then, they should be after you set targets in this step.

"Let me say first that I appreciated being invited to be part of Pioneer High School's improvement team. I believe we all have a stake in ensuring that our young people develop the skills that will enable them to become productive workers, good citizens, and confident adults. I don't have children myself, but all of us in the community have a responsibility to future generations. I've been involved in developing the PHS performance indicator system from the beginning, but felt most comfortable doing so during this current workshop on setting performance targets. As a businessman, I know this area well. I assess my own performance and that of my practice based on a set of performance targets I've identified. These include the total number of patients I see and total amount of revenue my office generates; the percent of business revenue coming from repeat customers and from referrals; and what I call my 'office utilization' rate, or the percent of available consultation hours that are booked with appointments. I felt I was able to contribute quite a bit at this step in the process. First, I shared my own experience in setting performance targets. For instance, while I always aim high, I sometimes have to reassess how quickly I can meet a target or rethink what I will have to do to meet it. Second, because I usually hire a high school student as an extra hand during the summer, I was able to help the team set specific performance targets for some of the work-related student outcomes we identified earlier on. To sum up, although I have always felt like a valued member of the school's improvement team, I felt like my contribution made a real difference to this step."

Chris Roberts, O.D. — Frontier Optometric Group

Performance Targets Are Specific and Measurable

In this chapter, you will assign specific and measurable targets to the indicators you identified in Step 3. For example, if you selected average daily attendance (ADA) rates or achievement test scores, you will now specify the performance level that you would like to obtain on these indicators. You may decide to set a target of 95 percent attendance or an average test score of 350 (on a scale ranging from zero to 500). Performance targets, however, should not be arbitrary. Strategies to help you set targets thoughtfully are described in detail on the following pages.

In some cases, you may have already identified performance targets as part of setting goals in Step 1. For example, a goal of "increasing the high school graduation rate to at least 90 percent" contains the specific and measurable target of 90 percent. In many cases, however, education goals do not identify numerical performance targets. A goal of "achieving high academic standards" is a case in point. It describes the general student outcome that is desired, not the specific levels of performance that are expected. Steps 2 and 3 helped bring such descriptive goals closer to being measurable, by identifying the specific outcomes, practices, and inputs implied by the goal and by selecting indicators to measure them. Step 5 completes the measurement process by assigning performance targets to your indicators. In the second example, the general goal of high academic standards might be translated into performance targets of 350 on standardized reading, mathematics, and science tests, as illustrated on the next page.

Set performance targets to achieve a bountiful harvest.

Making Goals Measurable

At Your Fingertips Step	1. Establish Goals	2. Identify Related Outcomes, Practices, and Inputs	3. Determine Data Sources and Indicators	4. Examine the Data	5. Set Performance Targets
Example 1	Increase the high school graduation rate to 90 percent	High school graduation (outcome)	Student records (data source) and graduation rate (indicator)	The current high school graduation rate is 82 percent	Graduation rate of 90 percent
Example 2	Achieve high academic standards for all students	Reading, mathematics, and science achievement (outcomes)	Standardized test (data source) and average test scores (indicator)	Average reading score is 265; Average mathematics score is 278; Average science score is 273	Average score of 350 on each part of the test (equivalent to advanced levels of proficiency)

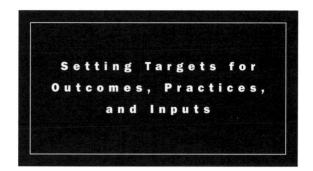

Performance targets provide specific goals to aim for and a means of measuring your progress and success. You can set targets for all of your performance indicators. However, it is most important to set targets for your outcome indicators, since these are the ultimate measure of your school's success. Setting the desired level of student performance in an area will help you both aim for your target and know when you have hit it.

In most cases, you may also find it useful to set performance targets for your practice indicators. Setting targets for related practices can be a primary strategy for achieving your outcomes. For example, in order to achieve your school's outcome target of an average science achievement test score of 350, you may set a practice target of having all students (100 percent) enroll in at least two years of laboratory science in high school. This practice target not only describes a concrete strategy for achieving the desired outcome but also

provides a means of evaluating the strategy. Your school may find that it achieves the 350-score target with only 80 percent of students enrolled in two years of laboratory science, or, in contrast, you may find that enrolling 100 percent of students in such courses fails to achieve the 350-score target. Setting performance targets for related practices can help you refine your improvement strategies.

Finally, you may also want to set targets for those input indicators over which you have some control. For instance, you might decide to reduce your student-teacher ratio from 22 to 17. Although reaching your target of 17 students per teacher may take considerable effort, setting this performance target could help generate a healthy discussion about how best to allocate staff resources at your school.

Setting performance targets involves asking the following questions:

· **How are you currently performing?**

· **What do you want to reach for?**

· **How will you get there?**

The rest of the chapter is organized around these three concerns.

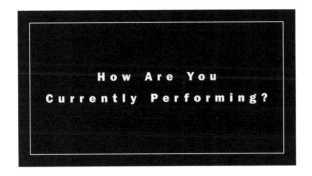

How Are You Currently Performing?

· **Compare your performance with that of an exemplary school or program.**

· **Compare your performance with state and national averages.**

· **Compare your performance with that of similar schools.**

In Step 4, you examined your indicator data with an eye toward understanding your performance within the context of your own school. The questions that concerned you focused on understanding the data themselves—where they came from, how they were compiled, what they meant in human terms, how they differed for important subgroups, and what significant relationships existed among them. In order to assess how you are currently performing, however, you may need to look beyond your school's context. Judging the adequacy of your performance often involves making external comparisons.

There are several possible ways to gather comparative information from external sources:

· **Review relevant state and national performance standards.**

· **Discuss expectations with important stakeholder groups.**

In the first two actions, you compare your performance against externally validated standards that all schools could be expected to meet. In the remaining examples, you compare your performance with that of other schools or programs. Comparing your school with exemplary schools or programs establishes a high standard to reach for, while comparing your school with average performers sets a more modest goal. Both strategies help you determine where your school lies in the grand scheme of things. In order to set fair performance targets, however, you may also want to compare your school to schools that have similar student demographics or other key resources and circumstances.

These sources of comparative information are discussed in detail below. You are encouraged to seek information from as many sources as is possible and practical.

Review Relevant State and National Performance Standards

Since the publication of *A Nation at Risk* in 1983 (National Commission on Excellence in Education 1983), a number of states, federal agencies, and national organizations have undertaken initiatives to establish performance standards in a wide variety of areas, such as the following:

- Performance standards associated with state competency and achievement tests and alternative assessments, such as New York's Regents Competency Test, the Texas Assessment of Academic Skills, the Kentucky Instructional Results Information System, and the Vermont Assessment Program.

- Performance standards associated with state-developed "school report cards," such as the Maryland School Performance Program and the California School Performance Report.

- State efforts to establish core performance standards and measures for evaluating vocational programs, as mandated by the 1990 Carl D. Perkins Vocational and Applied Technology Education Act.

- National academic skill standards projects, such as those undertaken by the National Council of Teachers of Mathematics and the National Academy of Sciences.

- National industry skill standards projects, as mandated by the 1994 National Skill Standards Act.

- Standards for the advanced certification of accomplished teachers, as promulgated by the National Board for Professional Teaching Standards.

These standards represent the levels of performance that developers believe to be crucial for success in subsequent education or in our contemporary society and economy. However, not all of the initiatives have produced numerical standards. While the first three initiatives cited above generally identify numerical performance standards, the latter three tend to describe their standards in narrative form. The narrative versions do not provide ready-made performance targets, but they may help you set targets by providing rich descriptions of desired levels of performance.

1. What types of performance standards are being used in your state or locality?

....

....

....

....

....

....

2. Which ones might be applicable to your school improvement efforts?

....

....

....

....

....

....

....

Discuss Expectations With Important Stakeholder Groups

To be meaningful, performance targets for your student outcomes should describe the skills, knowledge, and abilities that are necessary for success in subsequent education and as informed citizens and productive members of the work force. In order to identify the levels of performance students should strive to achieve, you may want to involve important stakeholder groups—such as local business representatives, postsecondary educators, parent and community groups—in setting your performance targets if they are not already part of your improvement team.

While participation of local stakeholders is useful for setting meaningful targets, it is not a substitute for broader-based efforts to establish performance standards. For example, local business representatives may have a sharp sense of their own skill needs, but may lack a broader labor market perspective. Nowadays people rarely stay in one job for an extended period of time. Since many change careers quite frequently—moving from one industry to another—the skills, knowledge, and abilities needed in these different industries sometimes change dramatically and rapidly. Thus, relying solely on a handful of local business people may not provide a complete picture of what graduates may need to know, achieve, or be able to do to be productive and flexible work force participants in the future. Moreover, preparing students for specific local jobs may not serve them well in the long run. Where possible, it is important for you to review the state and national initiatives described above that sought broad input in establishing their performance standards. However, involving local stakeholders in setting your performance targets remains important: they can provide useful and concrete elaboration of state and national standards and how they are applied locally.

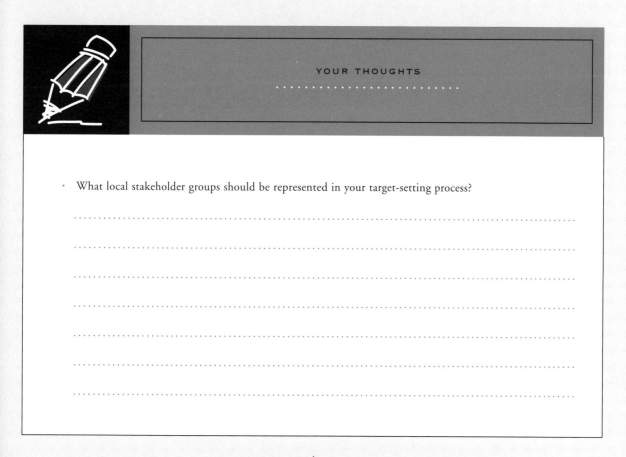

YOUR THOUGHTS

· What local stakeholder groups should be represented in your target-setting process?

Compare Your Performance With That of an Exemplary School or Program

You may find it helpful to compare your performance with that of an exemplary school or program, particularly where the above sources do not address the goals you identified in Step 1 or the outcomes you identified in Step 2. The process of identifying an exemplary school and studying how it achieves its success is called "benchmarking" (see Tucker 1996). You may want to select an exemplary school from schools that have similar demographics or other key resources. Through benchmarking, you can identify not only the level of performance that is realistic to achieve but also key practices that lead to success.

YOUR THOUGHTS

1. Which schools or programs are known for their exemplary performance?

....

....

....

....

....

....

....

2. How does your school's performance compare with theirs?

....

....

....

....

....

....

....

Compare Your Performance With State and National Averages

Finally, you can compare your school's performance on particular indicators with state and national averages for all schools or for schools with similar student populations. Perhaps the most readily available data on school performance are state and national standardized test results.[12] Some states and the U.S. Department of Education also publish data on other school performance indicators.[13] Information on the performance of similar schools provides a good comparison, if data are available to describe key resources (such as the socioeconomic make-up of the community served by the

school). Moreover, information on overall state and national averages provides a starting point for setting performance targets when other comparative information is not available to help identify similar schools. However, setting performance targets based solely on state and national averages—to the exclusion of the other sources of information described above—provides only modest assurances that the targeted level is externally valid or desirable.

[12] An example is the National Assessment for Educational Progress.

[13] Examples of these include state-developed school report cards and the *Condition of Education*, the annual statistical report of the National Center for Education Statistics.

YOUR THOUGHTS

1. What data are available to compare schools or programs in your state?

....
....
....
....
....

2. How well do these data help you identify schools with similar goals and resources?

....
....
....
....
....

After gathering comparative information on your school's performance from the above sources, you are ready to set performance targets. The course of action you decide to take will depend on how satisfied you are with your current performance and how persuasive the different sources of comparative information were in suggesting specific performance targets.

The following questions will help you set targets for the performance indicators you developed in Step 3.

· What specific performance target(s) did you identify in your search?

· Based on this information, how satisfied are you with your current performance on the indicator?

· If you discovered several different performance targets, which target do you think is the most appropriate given your circumstances?

· Over what period of time should you be able to reach your targeted performance level?

If you do not find information to support a specific performance target, you can choose instead to make incremental gains relative to your baseline data. For example, if your ADA rate is currently 80 percent—and you do not find information to describe either a state standard or average—you might decide to improve your performance by 10 percent and set an ADA target of 88 percent (80 + .10*80 = 88). You might also decide to apply this 10 percent improvement rate to all indicators that lack externally validated performance targets. Thus, if your current standardized reading test score is 265, you might set a test score target of 291.5 (265 + .10*265 = 291.5). Alternatively, you might decide to implement a 20 percent improvement rate, resulting in an ADA target of 96 percent, and a reading test score target of 318. However, this target-setting method is highly arbitrary. When at all possible, it is better to base your performance targets on levels that have been established by credible external sources.

Pioneer High School Target-Setting Example

Pioneer High School has a goal of raising the academic achievement of its students. With this in mind, stakeholders identified reading achievement as a specific outcome related to this goal and decided to assess that achievement based on a nationally available standardized reading test. Their baseline data revealed that the average reading test score for 12th graders was 265. In working toward achieving their goal, the team decided to gather information on performance targets from several sources.

Team members discovered that the national average for the reading test was 287, while the average for schools with similar student populations (based on parental education and level of economic disadvantage) was 275. Team members also examined the proficiency levels established by test developers: 1) "basic" reading corresponded to a score of 269; 2) "proficient" reading corresponded to a score of 304; and 3) "advanced" reading corresponded to a score of 348.

Team members were dissatisfied with their performance. The school's 12th graders were performing poorly on all fronts. For instance, their performance was lower than both the national average and the average for similar schools, and fell below the test's "basic" reading level. In response, some team members believed they should aim for the performance level of their peer institutions (a score of 275). After some discussion,

however, team members decided to set their performance target at 304, the "proficient" reading level on the test. They decided that this target accurately represented their hopes and expectations for their students—that all students achieve reading proficiency. They also agreed to revisit their performance target, leaving open the possibility of increasing it to the "advanced" reading level at some time in the future.

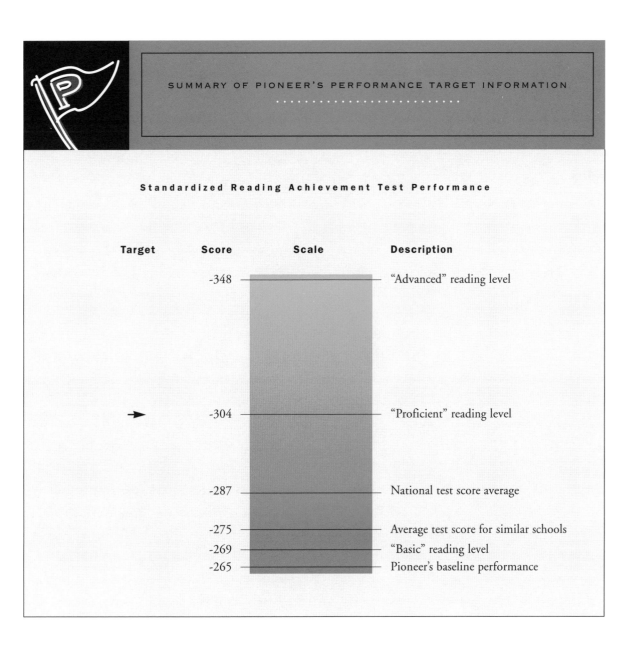

SUMMARY OF PIONEER'S PERFORMANCE TARGET INFORMATION

Standardized Reading Achievement Test Performance

Target	Score	Scale	Description
	-348		"Advanced" reading level
→	-304		"Proficient" reading level
	-287		National test score average
	-275		Average test score for similar schools
	-269		"Basic" reading level
	-265		Pioneer's baseline performance

Guidelines for Setting Performance Targets

The following are some general guidelines for setting performance targets for your indicators:

· *Set targets that are both realistic and incorporate high expectations.* Be wary of setting excessive targets that ensure failure, such as a graduation rate of 100 percent. Such targets may not be realistic. Plan to use your performance targets to motivate students and faculty to higher levels of achievement, not to intimidate or draw attention to meaningless milestones. Set a realistic target using one or more of the methods described above. These methods rely upon accepted information to guide target setting.

· *Understand what the target and its consequences mean in practical terms.* For example, what are the implications of increasing the average number of mathematics credits earned in high school from 2.6 to 3.0? What does achieving this target mean in practical terms? Although earning 3.0 credits in high school mathematics sounds like a reasonable target, it may be helpful to translate this target into course-taking behavior. Increasing the average number of mathematics credits earned from 2.6 to 3.0 means that 40 percent of students would have to complete an additional mathematics course. Or, 20 percent of students would have to complete two additional mathematics courses. Seen in this light, attaining an average of 3.0 mathematics credits requires changing the current course-taking behavior of students significantly, which you may or may not consider to be an attainable target for your school. Nevertheless, translating your performance targets from statistics into concrete terms can help you make this judgment. When the implications and consequences of a performance target are fully understood, you will have a better sense of where to set it, because you will know what is reasonable to aim for and what performance really looks like at this level.

· *Decide upon a time frame to attain the targets.* Once you set your performance targets and consider what they mean in terms of changing student behaviors and school practices, you should then identify a time frame for attaining them. Increasing ADA from 80 to 88 percent may not be realistic in one year, but it may be achievable in five. It is possible to fall into the trap of being either over- or under-ambitious. However, deciding on a realistic time frame can help you pace your efforts to improve performance.

· *Review and update your targets periodically.* This chapter provides guidelines for setting valid and reasonable performance targets. Where possible, you are directed to seek information from a variety of sources, including state and national performance standards initiatives, important stakeholder groups, exemplary schools and programs, and state and national averages on performance indicators. In some cases, the only information you may have on which to base your targets is your baseline data. After weighing the available information, you will attempt to set realistic targets that also promote high expectations. As you monitor your performance on your indicators over time, however, you may decide that certain targets are set either too high or too low for your circumstances; that the time frame you established was either too long or too short; or that you need to update the information you have gathered from external sources. There are not necessarily any right answers in setting performance targets, and some trial and error may be involved.

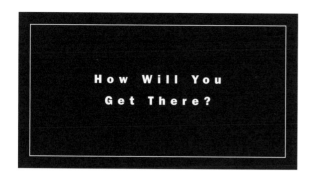

How Will You Get There?

Once you have set your performance targets, you will need to decide how best to achieve them. The following basic principles can help guide you in this endeavor:

· Discussion about improvement strategies should occur in the context of ongoing school improvement efforts.

· Change should be grounded in thoughtful analysis and careful planning.

Discussion Should Occur in the Context of Ongoing School Improvement Efforts

Over the last decade, there has been considerable discussion about how to improve the nation's schools. In response, schools have developed and implemented various improvement strategies. When interpreting your performance indicator data, you should proceed with this educational context in mind. Uncovering discrepancies between your actual and targeted performance should not lead you to adopt hasty new improvement strategies, and you should give careful thought to how existing improvement efforts can already help you attain your targets. As the old adage goes, "If it isn't broken, don't fix it!" The following questions can help you think about whether you will want to remain on the current course, modify existing strategies, or develop new ones:

· How satisfied are you that your current inputs, practices, and improvement strategies will help you attain your performance targets?

· What performance targets, if any, are not being addressed by current inputs, practices, and improvement strategies?

· What changes do you think need to occur in current inputs, practices, and improvement strategies in order to attain your targets?

Change Should Be Grounded in Thoughtful Analysis and Careful Planning

After some discussion, you may decide that improving your school's performance will require new or different strategies. Any changes that you make should be planned carefully. You can obtain information on possible improvement strategies from benchmarking exemplary schools and programs in your state or nationwide, from national professional organizations, school reform networks (such as the *Coalition of Essential Schools*, the *New American High Schools*, and the *High Schools That Work* network), state and national education agencies, and the educational research literature.

When planning your improvement strategies, keep the following questions in mind:

· What evidence exists to support the strategies you are considering?

· How confident are you that the proposed changes in inputs, practices, and improvement strategies will lead to improved performance on your indicators?

· Are the proposed changes consistent with your overall goals?

STEP

Set Performance Targets

Worksheets

Worksheets 5.1–5.3 will help you set performance targets and develop improvement strategies. Although the worksheets are written to accommodate teams, individuals can complete the activities on their own.

First, obtain copies of completed Worksheets 4.1A–C for each of your education goals. These worksheets contain your notes about your performance on your outcome, practice, and input indicators. If you are working as part of an improvement team, divide into small groups of three to five people, with each group selecting one or more goals.

Before completing Worksheet 5.1, you will need to gather comparative information by reviewing relevant state and national performance standards, discussing expectations with important stakeholder groups,

comparing your performance with that of an exemplary school or program, or comparing your performance with state and national averages. Before completing Worksheet 5.2, you will need to gather information on appropriate improvement strategies from efforts to benchmark exemplary schools or programs in your state or nationwide, national professional organizations, school reform networks, state and national education agencies, or educational research literature.

5.1 — Evaluating Performance on Your Outcome Indicators

Helps you summarize information and think critically about possible performance targets.

5.2 — Developing Improvement Strategies

Helps you to think critically about appropriate improvement strategies.

5.3 — Summarizing Performance Targets

For each goal, provides space to list your outcome, practice, and input indicators and your baseline data, performance targets, and projected time frames.

Goal ....

1. Review all of your copies of Worksheet 4.1A for the above goal, then copy your outcome indicators and the current level of performance on them below. Do not fill in your targets yet.

Outcome Indicators	Current Performance	Your Target

2. After gathering information about desirable levels of performance on the above outcome indicators, summarize below what you learned from

State and national performance standards: ....

....

....

....

Input from important stakeholder groups: ....

....

....

....

Exemplary school or program performance: ....

....

....

....

State or national averages: ....

....

....

....

3. Based on your research, answer the following questions, and then fill in your proposed performance targets for each outcome indicator:

What specific performance targets did you identify in your search? . . . .

. . . .

. . . .

. . . .

. . . .

Based on the information you gathered, how satisfied are you with your current performance on the above indicators?

. . . .

. . . .

. . . .

. . . .

If you discovered several different performance targets, what do you believe is the most appropriate target given your circumstances? . . . .

. . . .

. . . .

. . . .

4. After proposing performance targets, discuss the following and revise your targets as necessary:

Is the target realistic and does it incorporate high expectations? . . . .

. . . .

. . . .

What does the target mean in practical terms? Is this reasonable? . . . .

. . . .

. . . .

What time frame is realistic for attaining the targets? . . . .

. . . .

. . . .

. . . .

Goal . . . .

1. Review the performance targets you proposed in Worksheet 5.1 as well as Worksheets 4.1B and C for the above goal, and then discuss the following with your team:

How satisfied are you that your current practices and improvement strategies will help you attain the performance targets listed on Worksheet 5.1? . . . .

. . . .

. . . .

What performance targets, if any, are not being addressed by current practices and improvement strategies?

. . . .

. . . .

What changes do you think need to occur in current inputs, practices, and improvement strategies in order to attain the targets? . . . .

. . . .

. . . .

. . . .

2. Consider the following questions to help plan an appropriate course of action:

What evidence exists to support the improvement strategies you are considering (for example, from exemplary schools and programs, national professional organizations, school reform networks, state and national education agencies, and the educational research literature)? . . . .

. . . .

. . . .

How confident are you that the proposed changes in inputs, practices, and improvement strategies will lead to improved performance on your indicators? . . . .

. . . .

. . . .

Are the proposed changes consistent with your overall goals?

. . . .

. . . .

. . . .

For each goal, list your outcome, practice, and input indicators and corresponding baseline data, performance targets, and projected time frames. Then summarize your related improvement strategies in the space provided.

GOAL:

Priority Indicators	Baseline	Target	Time Frame
Outcome Indicators			
Practice Indicators			

Worksheet 5.3 continued

Priority Indicators	Baseline	Target	Time Frame
Input Indicators			

Summary of improvement strategies for this goal:

NEXT STEPS

Be sure to keep completed copies of Worksheet 5.3 for each of your education goals
so that you can refer to them in the future.

You are now ready to establish procedures to support continuous improvement at your school.

Step 6 | Monitor Performance Over Time

Congratulations! You have reached the final step of the *At Your Fingertips* model. Now you are ready to put

procedures in place that ensure your hard work will pay off in the long run. This step helps you establish a

system for collecting data on an ongoing basis, interpreting trends in your performance, and continuing improve-

"As the principal of Pioneer High School, I'm supposed to make sure things run smoothly. One of the reasons I really liked Step 6 is that it helped us develop a practical plan to support continuous improvement. It gives me confidence that the work we've put into *At Your Fingertips* will pay off later on. This should not be another fly-by-night reform effort. · At the beginning, some of my teachers saw this project as just another thing to do on top of everything else they're expected to do. Now that the hard part is over, we all think that our time has been well spent. After Step 6, we will have our performance indicator system in place and can begin monitoring our performance on a regular basis. · Soon, we will begin to see some progress on our indicators. Even if we don't make progress in all areas, the fact that we've set up this system demonstrates that we take our performance seriously. Already, I've had some good feedback from board members and parents who think we really should be commended for our efforts. By showing our willingness to be held accountable, we have boosted trust and goodwill in the community. I think the community may also be more willing now to participate in helping us achieve our goals."

Dr. Pat Wilson — Principal, Pioneer High School

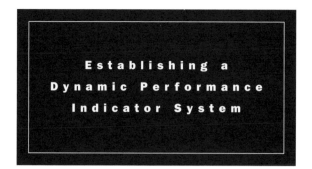

Establishing a Dynamic Performance Indicator System

Now that you have completed Steps 1–5 in this workbook, you have established education goals, developed performance indicators, examined your baseline data, and set performance targets. You have invested a lot of time and effort in creating a performance indicator system that provides useful and relevant information. You must now make sure your system is a dynamic one—that it continues to produce useful information over time and changes as your information needs change.

A dynamic performance indicator system helps you …

· **Collect important data on an ongoing basis.**

· **Interpret trends in your performance.**

· **Sustain or modify improvement efforts.**

Chart your growth over time for continuous improvement.

Monitor Performance Over Time

Collecting Data
on an Ongoing Basis

In Step 4, you collected and examined baseline data for most of your performance indicators. In order to measure your progress toward reaching your performance targets, you will need to collect, report, and examine your data periodically. Planning ongoing data collection activities requires that you ...

· **Set priorities among ongoing data collection efforts.**

· **Determine the frequency of data collection and analysis.**

· **Decide how to store your data.**

· **Assign roles and responsibilities for key tasks.**

Setting Priorities Among Ongoing Data Collection Efforts

As you set priorities among your ongoing data collection efforts, consider the following:

· *Decide which indicator data are the most important for understanding your progress toward achieving your education goals.* Some time has elapsed between Steps 1 and 6. Before setting priorities among your ongoing data collection efforts, you may want to review your education goals and confirm the performance indicators that offer the most useful and relevant information for understanding your progress toward reaching these goals.

· *Improve your indicator data.* While examining your baseline data in Step 4, you may have identified ways to improve the data. You may have decided that an indicator should be formulated differently or should be added or dropped, or that data collection or reporting procedures should be modified. For instance, rather than looking at average test scores, you may have decided that it was more informative to look at the percent of students scoring at or above proficiency levels, or to look at both types of indicators. When looking at average daily attendance (ADA) rates, for example, you may have decided that your school needed to improve the quality of classroom attendance records in order to improve the reliability of the data. Thus, collecting ADA on an ongoing basis may require concurrent efforts to improve attendance records.

· *Phase in new data sources.* In Steps 3 and 4, you may have identified new data sources that could provide crucial information not available from existing sources. For instance, you might want to augment your standardized test data with performance demonstrations to see how well students can apply their knowledge and skills to an authentic task. When phasing in new data sources, you will need to weigh how much time and resources you have to invest to develop the data source against how useful the new information will be to you.

· *Keep the data manageable.* Be realistic about how much data you can collect and review on an ongoing basis and consider the budgetary implications of carrying out your data collection plan. Remember that it may be better to start small and phase in new data slowly.

· What performance indicators should be given priority at your school and why?

....

....

....

....

....

....

....

Determining the Frequency of Data Collection and Analysis

After deciding on a list of priority indicators for future efforts, you will need to determine how frequently to collect and examine the data. You may need different schedules for your data. For example, standardized test scores may be reported once a year, while grades are awarded quarterly. Or, you may want to use some data in several ways. For example, you may want to examine grades on a quarterly basis in order to identify as early as possible students who are at risk of failing multiple courses or of not graduating, as well as look at grade data annually to determine the general course-taking patterns or grade distributions of your students.

As you plan your data collection and analysis schedule, consider the following factors:

· *Data availability.* Some data are available only infrequently—once a semester or once a year—while others are available on a regular, even daily, basis. Simply because the data are available, however, does not mean you need to collect or examine them immediately or repeatedly. In order to streamline your efforts, you may want to time your analysis to the availability of key data. In any case, you should be clear about the purposes behind the data collection and analysis schedule you set.

· *Data quality.* The frequency and timing of data collection can influence data quality. For example, collecting information about teachers' instructional practices on a quarterly basis may produce more accurate data than asking teachers to recall the practices they used over an entire school year. However, too frequent data collection can threaten data quality. For example, collecting data on teachers' instructional practices on a weekly basis can place too much of a burden on respondents, who may be less careful in their reporting or may feel pressure to distort the data.

- *Uses of the data.* How you plan to use your data may influence the frequency of your data collection and analysis. Data that can help you make small, continuous adjustments in your practices or improvement efforts need to be collected and examined more frequently than data that are used for more general analysis and long-term planning.

- *Local decision making.* Data collection and analysis should be timed to inform important school decisions about budgets, staffing, class scheduling, and so on. Parents and other stakeholders may also have information needs with particular timing concerns. For instance, parents may want an early warning if their children are not going to satisfy minimum college or university entrance requirements. Some of your data may already be reported at crucial times.

- *Time frames for achieving your performance targets.* How quickly you expect to meet your performance targets may determine how frequently you collect and examine your data. For example, if you hope to increase attendance significantly in a single year, you may want to monitor ADA rates on a daily, weekly, or monthly basis. If, on the other hand, you are focusing on changes in student understanding that are likely to take some time to occur, you may set a longer time frame and examine your data once a semester or even annually.

YOUR THOUGHTS

- How frequently do you think your different performance indicator data should be collected and analyzed, and why?

....

....

....

....

....

....

....

Deciding How to Store Your Data

If your performance indicator system relies primarily on existing data sources, data storage may not be an important concern for you. However, as many who have worked with data know, storing and analyzing data can quickly become complicated. Anticipating your data storage needs can help prevent delays and mix-ups and protect the quality and completeness of the data for your projected analyses.

As you think about your data storage requirements, consider the following factors:

· *Individual student records.* Many schools maintain automated student records that contain information on the demographic and educational experiences of individual students, such as date of birth, gender, course enrollments, grades, and test scores. Having all of this information in a single computer file—or in linked files—will help you perform certain types of data analysis. For example, you may want to examine the relationship between course taking and test scores, or differences in course taking or achievement for boys and girls. If you do not have automated individual student records, analyzing such relationships can become difficult. To remedy this, you might consider entering pairs or lists of associated characteristics into a computerized spreadsheet program. Of course, the time associated with entering these data makes safe storage of the resulting data files a top priority. On the other hand, the time needed to prepare the files may preclude doing such analyses. These same concerns apply to analyses of associated teacher characteristics or other units of analysis (such as classrooms or courses). Depending on how important these analyses are to your performance monitoring, you may want to consider establishing automated individual records where they do not already exist.

· *Longitudinal data.* Many trend analyses use cross-sectional data—that is, data for different groups at different points in time. As an example, examining senior test score trends does not require special data storage capabilities. However, examining gains or trends for individual students (or other units of analysis) requires longitudinal data—that is, linking data from two or more points in time for the same persons. If such key data elements are not included in your existing automated individual records, you may want to consider adding them. Safely storing data files that have been specially created to support longitudinal analysis is crucial.

· *Where your data will be stored.* Many of your performance indicator data will probably be maintained as part of existing databases. Where this is not the case, consider who should have access to the data to update them and analyze results. Storing data in certain locations may limit access to them either because specialized expertise is required to read the files or because confidentiality concerns restrict access. It may make sense for some data to be stored centrally, while other data are decentralized. It may also make sense for different persons to take responsibility for storing raw data files and maintaining either the analysis files or printed results.

· *How long your data will be stored.* You will also need to decide the length of time you will need to store your raw data and analysis results. Maintaining raw data allows for flexibility of analysis, including trend analysis over time. However, your data storage capacity may be limited and you may need to choose between some short- and long-term information needs.

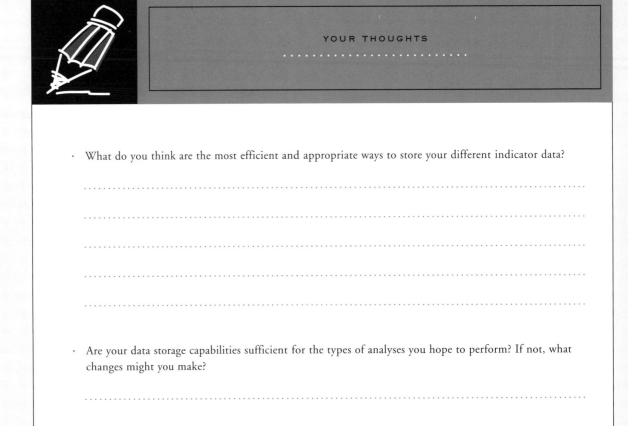

· What do you think are the most efficient and appropriate ways to store your different indicator data?

....

....

....

....

....

· Are your data storage capabilities sufficient for the types of analyses you hope to perform? If not, what changes might you make?

....

....

....

....

....

Assigning Roles and Responsibilities for Key Tasks

As a final step in planning your ongoing data collection and analysis activities, you should assign roles and responsibilities for key tasks to ensure that your plans proceed. Important roles and responsibilities include the following:

· Improving specific data collection and reporting practices.

· Developing new data sources.

· Collecting and compiling the data.

· Analyzing the data and reporting the results.

· Storing and updating the data.

Whom you assign to what task will depend on the following considerations:

· Confidentiality and security.

· Special expertise (in developing assessments, evaluation, databases, data analysis, desktop publishing, etc.).

· Special interest (in a particular performance area).

· Time availability.

Interpreting Trends in Your Performance

Once you establish procedures for collecting data on an ongoing basis you should begin to generate trend data. To help interpret trends in your performance over time, consider doing the following:

· *Graph your data.* Graphing your data will help you discern the direction and consistency of a trend. Indicating your performance target on the graph provides an indication of whether or not you are close to your target. In the example below, six years of ADA data are plotted, and the performance target of 95 percent ADA is included on the graph.

· *Note the direction and consistency of your trend data.* Is there a general or consistent trend in the data? Is the trend positive, negative, or holding steady? In some cases, your data may indicate a shifting trend. For instance, your data may hold steady for several years and then begin to move upward. In the example

below, there appears to be a slight upward trend in the ADA data, although there is some fluctuation from year to year.

· *Be cautious about concluding that a trend exists when you have only a few data points and the changes are small.* As the example below illustrates, data often fluctuate from one year to another without signifying a clear trend in performance. This random fluctuation may occur because of measurement error—that is, inaccuracy in data collecting and reporting. In the ADA example, the school would have been incorrect to conclude in 1992 that it had "significantly improved" its ADA rate over that in 1991. The school would also have been incorrect to conclude that its ADA rate "fell" in 1993 by a point. Rather, the small upward and downward adjustments in ADA suggest that there may be some measurement error associated with the ADA indicator and that "real" performance falls somewhere between the different measurements. However, if change persists over several years, then you can be more confident that you are experiencing a trend. This seemed to be the case over the six-year period from 1991 to 1996 because the ADA rate did appear to increase and approach the performance target of 95 percent.

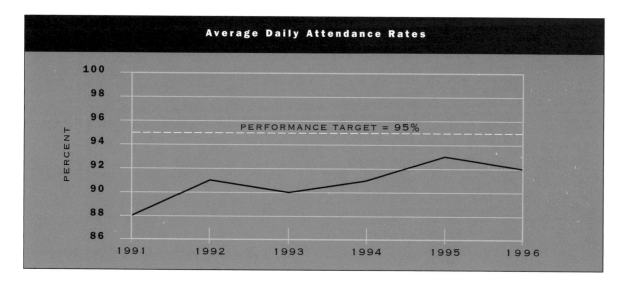

Average Daily Attendance Rates

Inside "The Black Box"

When you identify an upward trend in your data—particularly your outcome data—you may want to conclude that your improvement strategies caused the change. However, linking cause and effect is difficult to do, especially in a school setting where a complex mix of inputs and practices influence student outcomes. Similarly, a downward trend in the data may not be the result of failed improvement strategies. To help you investigate the factors affecting your student outcomes—in other words, to see into "the Black Box"—consider the following:

· *Decide to what you attribute the trends in your data.* What factors might have contributed to the results you are observing? What important inputs or practices have changed and could have influenced your performance? What improvement strategies may have contributed to the observed trends?

· *Determine how your improvement strategies have been implemented.* If you believe your improvement strategies might be responsible—at least in part—for your observed trends, you should determine whether and how they were implemented. Has your school implemented the improvement strategies the way they were intended? Have teachers changed their instructional practices or simply renamed them? Do all teachers define the new practices or improvement strategies in the same way? Is the school supporting implementation of the new practices or improvement strategies in the manner initially planned?

· *Decide how confident you are that your improvement strategies are either working or failing.* Do you have enough information to understand the trends in your data? What additional information do you need? Is there strong evidence to support changing your current course of action?

To find answers to some of these questions, you may need to observe or interview teachers and administrators in order to learn how they have implemented a new practice or strategy. In addition, you could survey students, teachers, and parents to find out whether they agree about a strategy's definition or expected student outcomes, and to ask them about their view of the impact of key practices on outcomes.

Supporting Continuous Improvement

Once your indicator system begins to produce performance data, you will need to communicate your progress to important stakeholder groups on a regular basis. Periodically, you will also need to revisit the six steps in the *At Your Fingertips* model in order to ensure that your system continues to produce useful and relevant information.

Communicating Your Progress

Communicating your school's progress regularly to important stakeholder groups is important for supporting continuous improvement efforts. Stakeholders can help interpret trends in performance, evaluate improvement strategies, and support improvement efforts. Alternatively, not communicating with important stakeholder groups can result in resistance to change or inertia.

When developing an organized communication strategy, consider the following factors:

· *Audience.* First, you should decide to whom you need to communicate your findings. Who might be affected by the findings? Who has a particular interest in a set of indicators or in how your school is meeting the performance targets for its goals? Consider stakeholders both inside and outside your school. You may identify multiple audiences with different interests.

· *Purpose.* After deciding who your audiences are, you should then clarify the purpose in communicating

your findings to them. Your primary purpose may be to solicit their help in interpreting the data or developing or implementing improvement strategies. You may want to generate a healthy discussion about alternative strategies, or you may be seeking approval for strategies you have already proposed. You may also hope to mobilize resources to meet your performance targets. Alternatively, you may want to communicate information as a public relations or marketing strategy—to get others interested in your school and thinking favorably about it.

· *Forum.* Depending on your audience and purpose, you will need to decide what the appropriate forum is for communicating your progress. Alternative forums include informal meetings, panel discussions, formal presentations, and written products, such as a school report card, newsletter, or school improvement report or plan. Decide if it is best to communicate your findings in a written format or verbally. Perhaps a combination of both approaches may be best, such as an oral presentation accompanied by visual aids. For more information on visual options for presenting data, refer back to Step 4.

· *Schedule.* When and how often should you communicate your progress to your different audiences? You may want to communicate your initial findings through a formal presentation, and then follow up with an annual progress report that includes a school report card. Alternatively, you may want to communicate informally on a more frequent basis. You may decide on different schedules for different audiences.

· *Content.* What do your audiences want and need to know? Consider including any background or supporting information your audience might need to understand the data or how they concern them.

· Who are your most important audiences, and how should you communicate your school's progress to them?

....

....

....

....

....

....

....

....

....

Revisiting the Six Steps

In order to ensure that your performance indicator system continues to produce useful information over time, it is important to revisit periodically the six steps of the *At Your Fingertips* model and to modify your system as necessary. As time passes, your school's goals may change, new data sources may become available, or you may decide that some performance indicators are more reliable or relevant than others. Alternatively, you may realize that your performance targets are set too high or too low and need to be adjusted, or that certain reporting formats or schedules could be improved.

Periodically—perhaps once a year or so—you may want to review the following list of questions and consider making any necessary modifications to your performance indicator system:

· Have your school's education goals or improvement strategies changed?

· Have any new data sources become available or old ones become obsolete?

· Should you eliminate, add, or reformulate any performance indicators to make them more reliable or relevant?

· Should any performance targets be reset, either because they have already been met or they are unrealistic?

· Do you need to modify your improvement strategies, either because some have proven to be ineffective or counterproductive, or because evidence suggests a new approach is called for?

· Do your data collection and storage procedures need to be modified?

· Has the schedule for collecting and examining your data and communicating your findings been working well or does it need to be modified?

· Has communication with your different stakeholder groups been effective or does your communication strategy need to be revised?

· Have any other problems related to implementing or using your performance indicator system been identified?

Worksheets

Worksheets **6.1–6.4** will help you establish a performance indicator system that supports continuous improvement. Although the worksheets are written to accommodate teams, individuals can complete the activities on their own.

First, obtain copies of completed Worksheets 2.3, 3.1, 3.4, 4.2, and 5.3 for each of your education goals. If you are working as part of an improvement team, divide into small groups of three to five people, with each group selecting one or more goals.

6.1 — Planning Ongoing Data Collection Activities
Helps you review the development of your indicators, decide on a final list of priority indicators for ongoing data collection purposes, plan the timing of your data collection and analysis, and decide where the data will be stored.

6.2 — Building Your Data Collection and Storage Capacity
Helps you identify indicators, data sources, and data stores that need to be improved or developed and devise a plan for building your capacity in these areas.

6.3 — Interpreting Trends in Your Performance
Provides you with a sample report card format, and helps you identify and interpret trends in your performance.

6.4 — Communicating Your Progress
Helps you develop an organized communication strategy.

6.5 — Revisiting the Six Steps
Provides a checklist for periodically revisiting the six steps in the *At Your Fingertips* model and revising your performance indicator system as needed.

This worksheet helps you review the development of your indicators, decide on a final list of priority indicators for ongoing data collection purposes, plan the timing of your data collection and analysis, and decide where the data will be stored.

1. Write down the education goal you are working on below.

2. Review the following worksheets related to this goal: 2.3—Finalizing Your Related Outcomes, Practices, and Inputs; 3.4—Developing a Final List of Outcome, Practice, and Input Indicators; and 4.2—Summarizing Your Findings, especially Part 4 on improving your indicator data. Decide which indicators are most important for understanding your progress toward achieving your goal, and list them in priority order in the appropriate outcome,

practice, or input section below or on the next page. Be realistic about how much data you can collect and review on an ongoing basis, and list only the most important indicators.

3. Think about the timing of data collection and analysis for each of your indicators, and note your suggestions below. Consider when the data usually become available; how the timing of data collection could influence data quality; how frequently the data should be reviewed to support ongoing adjustments in practices or long-term planning; when important local decisions are made; and the time frames you set in Worksheet 5.3 for achieving your performance targets.

4. Decide where the data should be stored to facilitate updating and analyzing these data and to respect confidentiality concerns.

GOAL:

Priority Outcome Indicators	Timing of Data Collection/Analysis	Data Storage Location
1.		
2.		
3.		
4.		
5.		
6.		
7.		
8.		
9.		
10.		

Worksheet 6.1 continued

Priority Practice Indicators

	Priority Practice Indicators	Timing of Data Collection/Analysis	Data Storage Location
1.			
2.			
3.			
4.			
5.			
6.			
7.			
8.			
9.			
10.			

Priority Input Indicators

	Priority Input Indicators	Timing of Data Collection/Analysis	Data Storage Location
1.			
2.			
3.			
4.			
5.			
6.			
7.			
8.			
9.			
10.			

This worksheet helps you identify indicators, data sources, and data stores that need improving or developing, and devise a plan for building your capacity in these areas.

1. Write down the education goal you are working on below.

2. Review Worksheet 4.2—Summarizing Your Findings, which is related to this goal. Especially review Part 4 on improving your indicator data. Identify any existing indicators or data sources that need to be improved, and list these in the first column of Part A. Decide what needs to be done (such as standardizing key definitions or data collection and reporting practices to make the data more reliable; who will be responsible; and what your target date is for completing this work.

3. Review all copies of Worksheet 3.1—Identifying Data Sources, which is related to this goal. In combination with Part 4 of Worksheet 4.2, identify any crucial

new data sources or indicators that need to be developed, and list these in the first column of Part B. Decide what needs to be done (such as forming a committee to develop the source, researching appropriate data collection and scoring methods, and developing survey or test items); who will be responsible; and what your target date is for completing this work.

4. Review the rest of Worksheet 4.2 and decide what types of analyses you want to perform that are related to this goal. In particular, consider whether you need to keep records for individual students (or teachers or others) or maintain longitudinal data (that is, two or more data points for the same students or others obtained at different points in time). Decide what stores of data need to be modified or developed, and list these in the first column of Part C. Describe what needs to be done (such as developing an automated individual record system or adding data elements to an existing one); who will be responsible; and what your target date is for completing this work.

GOAL:

A. Existing Indicators or Data Sources Needing Improvement	What Needs to Be Done?	Person(s) Responsible	Target Date
1.			
2.			
3.			
4.			

Worksheet 6.2 continued

B. New Indicators or Data Sources Needing Development

	What Needs to Be Done?	Person(s) Responsible	Target Date
1.			
2.			
3.			
4.			

C. Data Stores Needing Improvement or Development

	What Needs to Be Done?	Person(s) Responsible	Target Date
1.			
2.			
3.			
4.			

This worksheet helps you identify and interpret trends in your performance.

1. Write down the goal you are working on in the space provided on the following sample report card.

2. Copy your priority performance indicators related to this goal from Worksheet 6.1 and place them in the left-hand column of the report card.

3. Copy your performance targets from Worksheet 5.3 and place them in the right-hand column of the report card. (If you have added indicators in Step 6, you may need to set performance targets for them using Worksheet 5.1.)

4. Fill in your baseline data and any trend data you have collected up to now. Add successive data points as they become available. Space is provided for five years of performance data. In order to interpret your entire performance on a goal, you should analyze all of your related indicators at the same time. The assumption made here is that you review your entire performance on a goal annually, although you may choose to do so using a different time interval (such as once a semester or once every two years). In addition to this effort, you may also choose to review your performance on individual indicators at various times, as recorded in Worksheet 6.1.

5. Beginning with your outcome data, you may want to graph any important or interesting indicators.

6. For each outcome indicator, note the direction and consistency of the trend. Is there a general or consistent trend in the data? Is the trend positive, negative, or holding steady? Is there a break in the data, indicating that a trend is changing its direction?

. . . .

. . . .

. . . .

. . . .

. . . .

. . . .

7. For each outcome indicator, how confident are you that a trend exists? How many data points do you have to date? How large are the year-to-year changes? To what extent might these changes be due to measurement error? What might be sources of inaccuracy in collecting or reporting these data?

. . . .

. . . .

. . . .

. . . .

. . . .

. . . .

8. If you are confident that a trend exists in your outcome data, what do you think might help explain this trend? What changes in key inputs or practices or what specific improvement strategies do you think may be responsible for it? What evidence is there among your practice and input indicator data to support your hypotheses?

....

....

....

....

....

....

9. Are your outcomes moving in different directions? What might explain this?

....

....

....

....

10. Do you have enough information to understand the trends in your data? What additional information do you need?

....

....

....

....

11. You may want to investigate whether your school has implemented key improvement strategies in the way that was intended. Have teachers changed their instructional practices? Do all teachers define the improvement strategies in the same way? Is the school supporting implementation of the improvement strategies in the manner initially planned?

....

....

....

....

12. Is there strong evidence to support changing your current course of action? If so, what do you think needs to be done?

....

....

....

....

Sample Report Card						
GOAL:						
Performance Indicators	Year ___	Year ___	Year ___	Year ___	Year ___	**Target**
Outcome Indicators:						
Related Practice Indicators:						
Related Input Indicators:						

This worksheet helps you develop an organized communication strategy.

1. Decide who your audience(s) should be. Who would be interested in your general performance or in your performance on a specific goal or indicator? Who might be affected by your findings? Consider stakeholders both inside and outside your school. You may identify multiple audiences with different interests.

....

....

....

2. Decide what your purpose is in communicating your progress to each of your audiences. What do you hope to get out of this effort?

....

....

....

3. Decide what the appropriate forum is for communicating your progress to each audience (for instance, an informal meeting, panel discussion, formal presentation, school report card, newsletter, or school improvement report). Decide if it is best to communicate your findings in a written format, verbally, or both.

....

....

....

....

4. Decide when and how often you should communicate your progress to your different audiences.

....

....

....

5. Decide what the content of your presentation or product should be. What do your audiences want and need to know? What background or supporting information will help your audiences understand the data?

....

....

....

....

This worksheet helps you revise your performance indicator system so that it continues to produce useful information over time and supports continuous improvement at your school. Periodically, you should consider the following questions and determine whether you need to revisit any of the six steps in this workbook.

	Yes/Maybe	No/Unlikely
· Have your school's education goals changed?	☐	☐
If yes or maybe, return to Step 1 and work forward.		
· Have your improvement strategies changed?	☐	☐
If yes or maybe, return to Step 2 and work forward.		
· Have any new data sources become available or old ones become obsolete?	☐	☐
If yes or maybe, return to Step 3 and work forward.		
· Should you eliminate, add, or reformulate any performance indicators to make them more reliable or relevant?	☐	☐
If yes or maybe, return to Step 3 and work forward.		
· Should you reset any performance targets, either because they have already been met or are unrealistic?	☐	☐
If yes or maybe, return to Step 5 and work forward.		
· Do you need to modify your improvement strategies, either because some have proven to be ineffective or counterproductive or because evidence suggests a new approach is called for?	☐	☐
If yes or maybe, return to Step 5 and work forward.		
· Do you need to modify your data collection and storage procedures?	☐	☐
If yes or maybe, return to Step 6.		
· Has the schedule for collecting and examining your data and communicating your findings been working well or should you modify it?	☐	☐
If yes or maybe, return to Step 6.		
· Has communication with your different stakeholder groups been effective or do you need to revise your communication strategy?	☐	☐
If yes or maybe, return to Step 6.		
· Have you identified any other problems related to implementation or use of your performance indicator system?	☐	☐
If yes or maybe, return to Step 6.		

Be sure to keep completed copies of the worksheets from this step
so that you can refer to them in the future.

Congratulations! You have now completed all six steps of the *At Your Fingertips* model
and should have established a system that will produce
performance data on an ongoing basis, help you interpret trends in your performance,
and support continuous improvement.

STEP

Monitor Performance Over Time

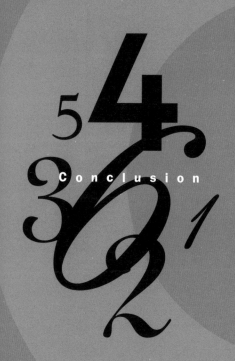

Conclusion

If you have reached this point in *At Your Fingertips*, you have probably learned quite a bit about how best to capture important aspects of your school's programs and goals in quantitative measures and about how to communicate such matters clearly and compellingly to colleagues and others in the community. More importantly, the questions you have asked yourself and the issues *At Your Fingertips* has pushed you to confront should spark a rich conversation about the important responsibilities your school has and about how it addresses them. Too often key considerations about the curriculum, pedagogy, resource allocation, and other crucial determinants of daily school operations go unexamined, as the crisis or fad of the moment captures everyone's attention. But these matters are central to the quality of education we provide the nation's children and to our interests in equal educational opportunity. Consequently, they deserve close attention by school people on an ongoing basis. They should not be assumed to be set in stone.

It is essential that schools find ways to periodically focus the collective energy and intelligence of the faculty, administrators, and others on the major factors that shape student learning. We set this as the threshold criterion for determining the value of *At Your Fingertips* to those who choose to take advantage of it. If it assists educators and the public in engaging in healthy discussion about their local schools, their goals, purposes, values, plans, and most importantly, results, it will have done its work.

Bibliography

Bickel, W.E. (1984). "Evaluator in Residence: New Prospects for School District Evaluation Research." *Educational Evaluation and Policy Analysis* 6 (3): 297–306.

Blank, R.K. (1993, April). *Developing a System of Educational Indicators: Selecting, Implementing, and Reporting Indicators.* Washington, DC: Council of Chief State School Officers.

Bottoms, G., and Mikos, P. (1995). *Seven Most Improved* High Schools That Work *Sites Raise Achievement in Reading, Mathematics, and Science.* Atlanta, GA: Southern Regional Education Board (SREB).

Braskamp, L.A., and Brown, R.D., eds. (1980). *Utilization of Evaluative Information.* New Directions for Program Evaluation Series, no. 5. San Francisco, CA: Jossey-Bass.

Bruininks, R.H. et al. (1991, July). *Assessing Educational Outcomes: State Activity and Literature Integration.* Minneapolis, MN: Minnesota University, National Center on Educational Outcomes.

Carl D. Perkins Vocational and Applied Technology Education Act of 1990. Public Law 101-392. 101st Cong., 25 September 1990.

Cohen, D.K., and Garet, M. (1975). "Reforming Educational Policy with Applied Research." *Harvard Educational Review* 45 (6): 17–43.

Cooley, W.W. (1983). "Improving the Performance of an Educational System." *Educational Researcher* 12 (6): 4–12.

Cousins, J.B., and Leithwood, K.A. (1986, Fall). "Current Empirical Research on Evaluation Utilization." *Review of Educational Research* 6 (3): 331–364.

Cronbach, L.J. and Associates. (1980). *Toward Reform of Program Evaluation.* San Francisco, CA: Jossey-Bass.

Cushman, K. (1996, January). "Documenting Whole-School Change in Essential Schools." *Horace* 12 (3): 1–7.

David, J.L. (1981, January/February). "Local Uses of Title I Evaluations." *Educational Evaluation and Policy Analysis* 3 (1): 27–39.

David, J.L. (1987, October). *Improving Education with Locally Developed Indicators.* Santa Monica, CA: RAND, Center for Policy Research in Education.

David, J.L. (1988, March). "The Use of Indicators by School Districts: Aid or Threat to Improvement?" *Phi Delta Kappan* 69 (7): 499–503.

Dickinson, K.P. et al. (1988, September). *Evaluation of the Effects of JTPA Performance Standards on Clients, Services, and Costs.* Washington, DC: National Commission for Employment Policy.

Dutton, M. et al. (1994). *The Tech Prep Resource Series: Evaluating Your Tech Prep Program.* Waco, TX: Center for Occupational Research and Development, Inc.

Fetler, M.E. (1994, October). "Carrot or Stick? How Do School Performance Reports Work?" *Education Policy Analysis Archives* 2 (13) (electronic journal).

Franklin, A.L., and Ban, C. (1994). *The Performance Measurement Movement: Learning from the Experiences of Program Evaluation.* Paper presented at the annual meeting of the American Evaluation Association, Boston.

Gardner, H. (1997, September). "Multiple Intelligences as a Partner in School Improvement." *Educational Leadership* 55 (1): 20.

Goals 2000: Educate America Act of 1994. Public Law 103-227. 103d Cong., 21 March 1994.

Haertel, E. (1986, May). "Measuring School Performance to Improve School Practice." *Education and Urban Society* 18 (3): 312–325.

Hanushek, E.A. (1994). *Making Schools Work: Improving Performance and Controlling Costs.* Washington, DC: The Brookings Institution.

Harp, L. (1995, February 15). "Kentucky Names Schools to Receive Achievement Bonuses." *Education Week* 14 (21): 11.

Herman, J.L., and Winters, L. (1992). *Tracking Your School's Success: A Guide to Sensible Evaluation.* Newbury Park, CA: Corwin Press, Inc.

Hoachlander, E.G., and Levesque, K.A. (1993). *Improving National Data for Vocational Education: Strengthening a Multiform System.* Berkeley, CA: National Center for Research in Vocational Education.

Hoachlander, E.G., Levesque, K.A., and Rahn, M.L. (1992). *Accountability for Vocational Education: A Practitioner's Guide.* Berkeley, CA: National Center for Research in Vocational Education.

Janis, I.L., and Mann, L. (1977). *Decision Making.* New York, NY: Free Press.

Job Training Partnership Act of 1982. Public Law 97-300. 97th Cong., 13 October 1982.

Job Training Reform Amendments of 1992. Public Law 102-367. 102nd Cong., 7 September 1992.

Kaagan, S.S., and Coley, R.J. (1989). *State Education Indicators: Measured Strides, Missing Steps.* New Brunswick, NJ: Rutgers University, Center for Policy Research in Education.

Kennedy, M.M. (1983, December). "Working Knowledge." *Knowledge: Creation, Diffusion, Utilization* 5 (2): 193–211.

Klausmeier, H.J. (1985). *Developing and Institutionalizing a Self-Improvement Capability: Structures and Strategies of Secondary Schools.* Lanham, MD: University Press of America.

Levesque, K., and Medrich, E. (1995). *School-to-Work Opportunities Performance Measures: First Year Data Collection.* Washington, DC: National School-to-Work Office, U.S. Departments of Education and Labor.

Lindblom, C.E., and Cohen, D.K. (1979). *Usable Knowledge.* New Haven, CT: Yale University Press.

McDonnell, L.M. et al. (1990, June). *Discovering What Schools Really Teach: Designing Improved Coursework Indicators.* Los Angeles, CA: Center for Research on Evaluation, Standards, and Student Testing.

McLaughlin, M.W., and Phillips, D.C. (1991). *Evaluation and Education: At Quarter Century.* Chicago, IL: National Society for the Study of Education.

Murnane, R.J., and Pauly, E.W. (1988, March). "Educational and Economic Indicators." *Phi Delta Kappan* 69 (7): 509–513.

National Commission on Excellence in Education. (1983). *A Nation at Risk.* Washington, DC: U.S. Government Printing Office.

National Study of School Evaluation. (1993). *Senior High School Improvement: Focusing on Desired Learner Outcomes.* Falls Church, VA: NSSE.

Nisbett, R., and Ross, L. (1980). *Human Inference: Strategies and Shortcomings of Social Judgment.* Englewood Cliffs, NJ: Prentice-Hall.

Oakes, J. (1986, October). *Educational Indicators: A Guide for Policymakers.* Santa Monica, CA: RAND, Center for Policy Research in Education.

Patton, M.Q. (1978). *Utilization-Focused Evaluation.* Beverly Hills, CA: Sage.

Porter, A. (1988, March). "Indicators: Objective Data or Political Tool?" *Phi Delta Kappan* 69 (7): 503–508.

Porter, A. (1991). "Creating a System of School Process Indicators." *Educational Evaluation and Policy Analysis* 13 (1): 13–29.

Rahn, M.L., Hoachlander, E.G., and Levesque, K.A. (1992). *State Systems for Accountability in Vocational Education.* Berkeley, CA: National Center for Research in Vocational Education.

Raizen, S.A., and Jones, L.V., eds. (1985). *Indicators of Precollege Education in Science and Mathematics: A Preliminary Review.* Washington, DC: National Academy Press.

Raizen, S.A., and Rossi, P.H., eds. (1981). *Program Evaluation in Education: When? How? To What Ends?* Washington, DC: National Academy Press.

Renihan, F.I., and Renihan, P.J. (1989). "School Improvement: Second Generation Issues and Strategies." In *School Effectiveness and School Improvement: Proceedings of the Second International Congress* (pp. 365–375). Eds. B. Creemers, T. Peters, and D. Reynolds. Rockland, MA/Berwyn, PA: Swets & Zeitlinger, Inc.

Richards, C.E. (1988, March). "Educational Monitoring Systems: Implications for Design." *Phi Delta Kappan* 69 (7): 495–498.

Rossi, P.H., and Freeman, H.E. (1993). *Evaluation: A Systematic Approach*. Beverly Hills, CA: Sage.

Sanders, J.R. (1992). *Evaluating School Programs: An Educator's Guide*. Newbury Park, CA: Corwin Press, Inc.

School-to-Work Opportunities Act of 1994. Public Law 103-239. 103d Cong., 4 May 1994.

Selden, R.W. (1988, March). "Missing Data: A Progress Report from the States." *Phi Delta Kappan* 69 (7): 492–494.

Selden, R.W. (1994). "How Indicators Have Been Used in the USA." In *Measuring Quality: Education Indicators: UK and International Perspectives*. Eds. K. Riley and D. Nuttall. London/Washington, DC: Falmer Press.

Senate Bill 1 of the 74th Texas Legislature, sec. 29.181, 30 May 1995.

Shavelson, R. et al. (1987). *Indicator Systems for Monitoring Mathematics and Science Education*. Santa Monica, CA: RAND.

Shavelson, R., McDonnell, L.M., and Oakes, J. (1989). *Indicators for Monitoring Mathematics and Science Education: A Sourcebook*. Santa Monica, CA: RAND.

Sizer, T.R. (1989). "Diverse Practice, Shared Ideas: The Essential School." In *Organizing for Learning: Toward the 21st Century*. Eds. H.J. Walberg and J.J. Lane. Reston, VA: National Association of Secondary School Principals.

Smith, M.S. (1988, March). "Educational Indicators." *Phi Delta Kappan* 69 (7): 487–491.

Southern Regional Education Board (SREB). *High Schools That Work* network. (1995). High Schools That Work *Site Development Guide #2: School Site Teams*. Atlanta, GA: Author.

Sproull, L.S., and Zubrow, D. (1982). "Performance Information in School Systems: Perspectives from Organization Theory." *Educational Administration Quarterly* 17 (3): 61–79.

Stecher, B.M., and Hanser, L.M. (1992). *Local Accountability in Vocational Education: A Theoretical Model and Its Limitations in Practice*. Berkeley, CA: National Center for Research in Vocational Education.

Stecher, B.M., and Hanser, L.M. (1993). *Beyond Vocational Education Standards and Measures: Strengthening Local Accountability Systems for Program Improvement.* Berkeley, CA: National Center for Research in Vocational Education.

Stecher, B.M. et al. (1995). *Improving Perkins II Performance Measures and Standards: Lessons Learned from Early Implementers in Four States.* Berkeley, CA: National Center for Research in Vocational Education.

Stern, D. (1986, May). "Toward a Statewide System for Public School Accountability: A Report from California." *Education and Urban Society* 18 (3): 326–346.

Timar, T.B., and Kirp, D.L. (1986). "Educational Reform and Institutional Competence." *Harvard Educational Review* 57 (3): 309–330.

Tucker, S. 1996. *Benchmarking: A Guide for Educators.* Thousand Oaks, CA: The Corwin Press.

U.S. Department of Education. National Center for Education Statistics. (1995). *Vocational Education in the United States: The Early 1990s* (NCES 95-024), by K.A. Levesque et al. Washington, DC: U.S. Government Printing Office.

U.S. Department of Education. National Center for Education Statistics. (1996a). *The Condition of Education 1996* (NCES 96-304), by T.M. Smith. Washington, DC: U.S. Government Printing Office.

U.S. Department of Education. National Center for Education Statistics. (1996b). *Descriptive Summary of 1989–90 Beginning Postsecondary Students: 5 Years Later* (NCES 96-155), by L.K. Berkner, S. Cuccaro-Alamin, and A.C. McCormick. Washington, DC: U.S. Government Printing Office.

U.S. Department of Education. Office of Educational Research and Improvement. (1988, September). *Creating Responsible and Responsive Accountability Systems.* Washington, DC: U.S. Government Printing Office.

U.S. Department of Education. Planning and Evaluation Service. (1997, April). "Partners in Progress: Early Steps in Creating School-to-Work Systems." Draft Report. Washington, DC.

Weiss, C.H. (1980). "Knowledge Creep and Decision Accretion." *Knowledge: Creation, Diffusion, Utilization* 1 (3): 381–404.

Zucker, L.G. (1980). *Institutional Structure and Organizational Processes: The Role of Evaluation Units in Schools.* Center for the Study of Evaluation (CSE) Report, no. 139. Los Angeles, CA: University of California, Los Angeles, CSE.

Appendices

Appendix A

STAKEHOLDER GROUPS

Why Involve the Following Stakeholder Groups?

TEACHERS · Teachers are directly responsible for what students learn in school. As part of an improvement team, teachers can help identify realistic learning goals, determine the reasons for poor performance in some areas, and develop workable improvement strategies. Since teachers may be responsible for implementing many improvement efforts, it is important to involve them as key members of an improvement team. By involving academic, vocational, and special education teachers, a team will be able to address all important learning objectives and the needs of all groups of students when shaping their vision for the school.

DEPARTMENT CHAIRPERSONS · These faculty representatives are in a strong position to communicate the concerns and suggestions of teachers in their departments to the improvement team, and to disseminate information from the team among faculty members. Since teachers' cooperation is crucial to the success of improvement efforts, department chairpersons are well positioned to act as intermediaries between a small improvement team and the entire faculty.

CAREER OR GUIDANCE COUNSELORS · Counselors are often responsible for administering a range of assessments, including achievement tests, college aptitude tests, and occupational interest inventories. Thus, they are not only knowledgeable about the many types of data sources available at a site but also are familiar with student performance. Counselors may also be aware of how students' personal interests and problems may contribute to their performance, and can suggest strategies for addressing the most common concerns.

CLASSIFIED SCHOOL STAFF MEMBERS · Staff members other than teachers, counselors, and administrators often assume key roles in the life of a school. Depending upon the scope of your improvement efforts, medical, social service, secretarial, media center, maintenance, and food service personnel can bring useful perspectives and contribute to the success of proposed improvement strategies.

SCHOOL ADMINISTRATORS · School administrators, including the principal and assistant principal(s), can be key players in mobilizing change in schools. Their involvement in improvement efforts can often lend legitimacy to the process and a sense of urgency. School administrators are also well positioned to help overcome barriers to implementation.

DISTRICT ADMINISTRATORS · District administrators, such as the superintendent and assistant superintendent, can contribute to an overall vision for the district. Because they are familiar with the common concerns in their jurisdiction, they can provide a strong link among schools. District administrators not only influence school-level priorities and can provide momentum to improvement efforts, but also maintain various data sources in the district office and can familiarize team members with these data and make them available to the team.

SCHOOL BOARD MEMBERS · School Board members can also contribute to an overall vision for a district or school, and they bring a community perspective to discussions about education goals. By participating in the program improvement process, Board members can learn more about the concerns of educators and other stakeholders and the rationale for improvement strategies. Moreover, participating Board members can represent findings and plans to other Board members. In some cases, Board members may be able to make funds available for the overall improvement process or for specific improvement efforts.

STATE EDUCATION AGENCY STAFF · State education agency staff have a broad perspective on education efforts in the state and can contribute fresh ideas to your school's discussion of goals, perceived problems, and potential solutions. Moreover, agency staff usually maintain a variety of education data in the state office and can familiarize team members with these data and make them available to them. In some cases, state agencies may be able to make funds available for improvement efforts.

STUDENTS · Students contribute a unique perspective to identifying problems and developing potential solutions. Particularly where problems and solutions necessitate understanding student motivation, they can provide valuable insights. Involving students also helps increase general student interest in improvement efforts.

PARENTS · Parents are important partners in the education process. Along with students, they are the chief "consumers" of education, and as such provide a vital perspective on education goals and strategies. Parents want to know what their school's strengths and weaknesses are, and have a vested interest in helping find ways to improve education outcomes. Parents can also help mobilize community resources in order to support improvement efforts.

EMPLOYERS · Employers in your locality and state have an important stake in how your district, school, or program performs. Whether they hire graduates directly out of high school or after some post-secondary education or training, employers depend on high school students obtaining a solid foundation of academic, critical thinking, and general employability skills. In some cases, employers also have an interest in assuring that high school students obtain specific occupational skills. As improvement team members, employers can contribute to discussions about desired education goals, student outcomes, and learning strategies. Moreover, they can provide a constructive link to the business community that may be essential if one of your school's strategies includes increasing work-based learning opportunities for students or encouraging other school/work linkages.

POSTSECONDARY EDUCATION REPRESENTATIVES · Representatives of postsecondary institutions in your locality and state can bring an important perspective to your school's improvement efforts. They not only have an interest in ensuring that high school graduates are adequately prepared for postsecondary work, but also are familiar with the entrance requirements and skills required for performing well and persisting in postsecondary education once students have enrolled. In addition, if secondary/postsecondary articulation agreements or tech-prep programs are part of your school's strategies, postsecondary education representatives can also help establish them.

OTHER COMMUNITY MEMBERS · Depending on local circumstances and your site's particular education vision, you may want to involve other community members in your improvement team. For example, you may want to consider recruiting labor representatives as team members. Labor representatives are knowledgeable about skill requirements in their industry and can provide a resource for teaching students about major industries and career opportunities in your area. As another example, your school may place a high value on having students learn through volunteer or service experiences. By involving large "employers" of volunteers or organizations that coordinate volunteer efforts, you can help clarify the education objectives of such experiences and improve the linkages between these experiences and school-based learning. You should carefully consider your own special circumstances when deciding whether to involve a wider group of stakeholders in your improvement team.

September 23, 1997

Dear _____ :

I am writing to invite you to join in an exciting and important endeavor. Pioneer High School is about to begin a multi-year school improvement process. We would like you to become a member of our improvement team.

Pioneer High School has a long and proud history of educating the young people of Frontier. However, while we believe that we are doing a good job, we have little in the way of hard data to back up our perceptions. The proposed school improvement project will develop a performance indicator system that will collect meaningful information about how well our school is functioning. This indicator system will also help us identify our strengths and weaknesses and develop improvement strategies. As a member of the improvement team, you will be involved in the entire process, from deciding what our school goals should be to identifying needed information, reviewing the findings, and developing and implementing improvement strategies.

Although the improvement project is a multi-year effort, the crucial building blocks will be put in place during the first year. As a team member, you could expect to devote about four hours per month to the project through the end of the current academic year. In future years, we will convene three or four times a year to monitor our progress and to continue improvement efforts.

We hope you will consider joining our team of teachers, administrators, students, parents, and community members. This is a unique opportunity to shape the future direction of our high school.

Please contact me or my secretary at (999) 555-1111 by October 9, if you are interested in learning more about the project. An orientation and information meeting will be held Wednesday evening, October 16, from 6 to 9 p.m. in the high school cafeteria. I have enclosed a tentative agenda for the meeting.

Thank you for your interest and support.

Sincerely,

Dr. Pat Wilson
Principal, Pioneer High School
1 Main Street
Frontier, XX 00000

Pioneer High School Improvement Project

Orientation and Information Meeting · Wednesday, October 16, 6 to 9 p.m. · School Cafeteria

I. Welcome and Introductions

II. Overview

    A. Need for developing a performance indicator system at PHS

    B. Potential benefits of developing a performance indicator system

    C. Description of the six-step process

    D. Discussion of expected time commitments

III. Workshop/Group Exercise

    A. Identify questions or concerns

    B. Determine who is present and whether additional recruitment efforts are needed

    C. Discuss team roles and responsibilities and ask for volunteers

    D. Develop a team meeting schedule

    E. Agree on team procedures and ground rules

IV. Question and Answer Period

V. Collection of names and contact information from people who are interested in actively participating as a team member

ALTERNATIVE ASSESSMENT

Allen, D. "The Tuning Protocol: A Process for Reflection." Contact the Publications Office of the Coalition of Essential Schools at (401) 863-3384.

Allen, D., and Mc Donald, J. "Keeping Student Performance Central: The New York Assessment Collection." Contact the Publications Office of the Coalition of Essential Schools at (401) 863-3384.

Herman, J.L., Aschbacher, P.R., and Winters, L. (1992). *A Practical Guide to Alternative Assessment.* Alexandria, VA: Association for Supervision and Curriculum Development (ACSD). Contact ACSD at (703) 549-9110.

Newmann, F.M., Secada, W.G., and Wehlage, G.G. (1995). *A Guide to Authentic Instruction and Assessment: Vision, Standards, and Scoring.* Contact the University of Wisconsin's Center on Organization and Restructuring of Schools at (608) 263-7575.

Niguidula, D. "The Digital Portfolio: A Richer Picture of Student Performance." Contact the Publications Office of the Coalition of Essential Schools at (401) 863-3384.

Washor, E. "Show, Don't Tell: Video and Accountability." Contact the Publications Office of the Coalition of Essential Schools at (401) 863-3384.

ATTITUDE SCALES

Robinson, J.P., Athanasiou, R., and Head, K.B. (1969). *Measures of Occupational Attributes and Occupational Characteristics.* Ann Arbor, MI: Institute for Social Research, University of Michigan.

Robinson, J.P., and Shaver, P.R. (1973). *Measures of Political Attitudes.* Ann Arbor, MI: Institute for Social Research, University of Michigan.

Robinson, J.P., and Shaver, P.R. (1973). *Measures of Social Psychological Attitudes.* Ann Arbor, MI: Institute for Social Research, University of Michigan.

Shaw, M.R., and Wright, J.M. (1967). *Scales for the Measurement of Attitudes.* New York, NY: McGraw-Hill.

DATA ANALYSIS

Anderson, G. et al. *Studying Your Own School: A Guide to Qualitative Practitioner Research.* Thousand Oaks, CA: Corwin Press. Contact Corwin Press at (805) 499-9734.

Fitz-Gibbon, C.T., and Morris, L.L. (1987). *How to Analyze Data.* Newbury Park, CA: Sage.

DOCUMENT ANALYSIS

Budd, R.W. et al. (1967). *Content Analysis of Communication.* New York, NY: Macmillan.

Guba, E.G., and Lincoln, Y.S. (1981). *Effective Evaluation.* San Francisco, CA: Jossey-Bass.

Holsti, O. (1969). *Content Analysis for the Social Sciences and Humanities.* Reading, MA: Addison-Wesley.

INTERVIEWS

Borg, W.R., and Gall, M.D. (1989). *Educational Research*. New York, NY: Longman.

Dillman, D.A. (1978). *Mail and Telephone Surveys: The Total Design Method*. New York, NY: John Wiley.

Fowler, F.J., Jr. (1989). *Survey Research Methods*. 2nd ed. Newbury Park, CA: Sage.

Fowler, F.J., Jr., and Mangione, T.W. (1990). *Standardized Survey Interviewing: Minimizing Interviewer-Related Error*. Newbury Park, CA: Sage.

Gorden, R.L. (1980). *Interviewing: Strategy, Techniques, and Tactics*. Homewood, IL: Dorsey.

OBSERVATION

Webb, E.J., Campbell, D.T., Schwartz, R.D., and Sechrest, L. (1966). *Unobtrusive Measures: Nonreactive Research in the Social Sciences*. Chicago, IL: Rand McNally.

QUESTIONNAIRES

Berdie, D., and Anderson, J. (1974). *Questionnaires*. Metuchen, NJ: Scarecrow.

Borg, W.R., and Gall, M.D. (1989). *Educational Research*. New York, NY: Longman.

Dillman, D.A. (1978). *Mail and Telephone Surveys: The Total Design Method*. New York, NY: John Wiley.

Fowler, F.J., Jr. (1989). *Survey Research Methods*. 2nd ed. Newbury Park, CA: Sage.

Fowler, F.J., Jr., and Mangione, T.W. (1990). *Standardized Survey Interviewing: Minimizing Interviewer-Related Error*. Newbury Park, CA: Sage.

SURVEYS

Borg, W.R., and Gall, M.D. (1989). *Educational Research*. New York, NY: Longman.

Dillman, D.A. (1978). *Mail and Telephone Surveys: The Total Design Method*. New York, NY: John Wiley.

Fink, A., and Kosecoff, J. (1985). *How to Conduct Surveys: A Step-by-Step Guide*. Newbury Park, CA: Sage.

Fink, A., ed. (1995). *The Survey Kit*. Newbury Park, CA: Sage.

Fowler, F.J., Jr. (1989). *Survey Research Methods*. 2nd ed. Newbury Park, CA: Sage.

Fowler, F.J., Jr., and Mangione, T.W. (1990). *Standardized Survey Interviewing: Minimizing Interviewer-Related Error*. Newbury Park, CA: Sage.

TESTING

Bloom, B., Hastings, J.T., and Madaus, G.F. (1971). *Handbook on Formative and Summative Evaluation of Student Learning*. New York, NY: McGraw-Hill.

Hopkins, K.D., and Stanley, J.C. (1981). *Educational and Psychological Measurement and Evaluation*. Englewood Cliffs, N.J: Prentice-Hall.

Duplicate Worksheets

On the following pages are black and white versions of all the worksheets contained in *At Your Fingertips*. These duplicates may be used for photocopying purposes provided the purchaser agrees to the following conditions.

This single-user site license gives the one person designated as the "Primary User" of this workbook permission to make copies of these worksheets for fair use, provided that 1) duplication is for an educational purpose in a not-for-profit institution; 2) the copies are made available without charge beyond the cost of reproduction; and 3) the copyright line appears on all copies.

The permission to copy does not 1) extend to copying this workbook in its entirety or copying any part for distribution to other sites; or 2) transfer to those persons given reproduced materials by the "Primary User."

A "site" is defined as a single location, such as a school or school district.

You can begin building an improvement team by completing the four activities that follow. The individual who is responsible for launching a performance indicator system at your school should fill out the worksheet before convening the first team meeting.

1. Decide what the scope of your improvement efforts will primarily be. Select one area for improvement, and then identify the district(s), school(s), program(s), department(s), or classroom(s) you hope will participate:

☐ District ....

☐ School ....

☐ Program ....

☐ Department ....

☐ Classroom ....

2. Who should be represented on your team? Check (√) all groups that apply, and list key individuals from each group who should be invited:

☐ Students ....

☐ Parents ....

☐ Teachers ....

☐ Department chairpersons ....

☐ Career or guidance counselors ....

☐ School administrators ....

☐ Other school staff ....

☐ District administrators ....

☐ School Board members ....

☐ Union leaders ....

☐ State education agency staff ....

☐ Employers ....

☐ Postsecondary education representatives ....

☐ Other community members ....

3. Who should be the team leader? ....

4. An invitation letter, conversation, or phone call should do the following things: (Space has been provided for you to jot down notes about what you might include in your invitation, and a sample invitation letter is included in Appendix B.)

Alert the reader to the upcoming project to develop a performance indicator system.

What will you call the project? ....

How can you get their attention? ....

Explain the need for the project.

....

....

Explain the benefits of being involved.

....

....

Briefly describe the project.

....

....

Describe the time commitment team members will be expected to make.

....

....

Specify the date, time, and location of an orientation and organizational meeting.

....

....

Explain the next step that prospective team members should take to demonstrate their interest.

....

....

You may want to enclose a copy of the Introduction along with the invitation letter to provide prospective participants with more information about the improvement process.

This worksheet should be completed by participants at the first team meeting. You can begin organizing your improvement team by completing the following five activities:

1. Use the space below to note any questions that you would like answered during the orientation and organizational meeting. Record responses to those questions as they arise.

. . . .

. . . .

. . . .

. . . .

2. Are there any stakeholder groups or persons missing from the meeting who would be a valuable addition to the team? Use the space below to identify them.

. . . .

. . . .

. . . .

. . . .

3. Discuss and record who will assume the following roles and responsibilities for your team:

Role   **Person Responsible**

Meeting facilitator (guides participants as they fill
out the worksheets and discuss important issues)   . . . .

Archivist (keeps copies of completed worksheets
and other documentation)   . . . .

Meeting organizer (reserves meeting room,
sends reminders)   . . . .

Other role . . . .

Other role . . . .

4. Decide when and where your improvement team will meet. You may want to refer to the suggested calendar for Year 1 on page 33 of this chapter for ideas.

· How frequently will the team meet? ....

· About how long will team meetings last? ....

· When will the next meeting be held (date and time)? ....

· Where will the next meeting be held? ....

· Does anything else need to happen before the next meeting? If so, what? Who will be responsible? ....

....

....

....

Team members should plan to read the chapter *Step 1—Establishing Goals* before the next meeting.

5. Determine what your team ground rules and operating procedures will be. As a group, discuss and answer the following questions:

· How will team decisions be finalized (consensus, voting, other)?

....

....

· How will team members communicate with each other (meetings, memos, e-mail, other)?

....

....

· How will team members communicate with non-members (staff meetings, newsletter, other)?

....

....

· Other rules or procedures? ....

....

....

Activities 1–9 in this worksheet will help you establish a set of education goals, for those who do not already have existing goals or who want to start the goal-setting process over again. (If you already have goals you would like to consider, skip to Worksheet 1.2.) If you are working as part of a team, your entire team should plan to complete this worksheet together in order to reach consensus on your goals.

1. Display or distribute copies of the following six criteria: "Goals should be meaningful, realistic, complementary, given clear priorities, agreed to by all stakeholders, and measurable."

2. As a **large group**, review the examples of goals provided on page 44. Goals should focus on student outcomes—what it is you want students to know, think, believe, value, achieve, or be able to do. Goals may be written in broad or specific terms, and may focus on all students or a subset of students.

3. **Individually**, think about what you believe are the most important education goals for your district, school, program, department, or classroom. Your goals should describe desired student outcomes. Record your ideas in the space below:

. . . .

. . . .

. . . .

. . . .

. . . .

4. Break up into **small groups** of three to five persons to share the goals you identified in Activity 3. Ask yourselves the following question: Which of these goals do we all value for our students? Record areas of agreement and disagreement below. If you have a long list of agreed-upon goals, check off the 10 goals that your small group considers most important, and designate a spokesperson who will describe these goals to the large group.

. . . .

. . . .

. . . .

. . . .

. . . .

. . . .

. . . .

. . . .

. . . .

5. Everyone returns to the **large group**. The designated spokesperson from each small group shares his or her group's goals (including areas of agreement and disagreement) with the large group. Then the large group identifies and discusses themes that are common among all the groups, and the facilitator records them and lists the different goal statements that fall under each theme. You may need to weed out some goals that do not focus on student outcomes.

6. Break up into different **small groups** of three to five persons (mixing up the membership of previous groups). The facilitator then assigns one or more thematic areas to each group, so that all themes are assigned. In your small group, review your theme and the related goal ideas, and then draft one or more goal statements to summarize your thematic area. Designate a spokesperson for your group.

   Your small group's theme(s): ....

   ....

   ....

   ....

   ....

   Summary goal statement(s): ....

   ....

   ....

   ....

   ....

7. Everyone returns to the **large group**. The designated spokesperson from each small group shares his or her group's goal statements with the large group. The facilitator then records the goal statements and displays them where everyone can see them.

8. As a **large group**, team members discuss any differences of opinions that may have come up over goal selection or wording and attempt to agree on a common set of goals.

9. In the space provided below, write down the final agreed-upon goal statement(s) for your small group's thematic area. The facilitator should record all of the final goal statements so they are available for future use.

   Final goal statement(s) for your thematic area: ....

   ....

   ....

   ....

   ....

   ....

   ....

   ....

➧ **Proceed to Worksheet 1.3**

Activities 1–9 in this worksheet help you review and revise your existing education goals. (If you do not have any existing goals, return to Worksheet 1.1.) If you are working as part of a team, your entire team should plan to complete this worksheet together in order to reach consensus on your goals. Before beginning the worksheet, your meeting facilitator should collect all sets of education goals that have already been established at your school. Goals may have been developed as part of other education initiatives, such as strategic planning efforts, conducting a community needs assessment, developing a new program, implementing a new curriculum, or as part of a grant application process.

1. Display or distribute copies of the following six criteria: "Goals should be meaningful, realistic, complementary, given clear priorities, agreed to by all stakeholders, and measurable."

2. As a **large group**, review the examples of goals provided on page 44. Goals should focus on student outcomes—what it is you want students to know, think, believe, value, achieve, or be able to do. Goals may be written in broad or specific terms, and may focus on all students or a subset of students.

3. Display or distribute copies of your school's existing goals.

4. Break up into **small groups** of three to five persons to review the existing goals. First, identify the goals that describe student outcomes, and focus on these. Then, ask yourselves the following questions:

· Which of these goals do we value most?

· Are there any goals that are less important?

· Are there any important goals that are missing?

Record areas of agreement and disagreement below. If you have a long list of agreed-upon goals, check off the 10 goals that your small group considers most important, and designate a spokesperson who will describe them to the large group.

· ·

5. Everyone returns to the **large group**. The designated spokesperson from each small group shares his or her group's modified goals (including areas of agreement and disagreement) with the large group. The large group then identifies and discusses themes that were common among all the groups. The facilitator writes down these themes and lists the different goal statements that fall under each theme. You may need to weed out some goals that do not focus on student outcomes.

6. Break up into different **small groups** of three to five persons (mixing up the membership of previous groups). The facilitator assigns one or more thematic areas to each group, so that all themes are assigned. In your small group, review your theme and its related goals, and then draft one or more goal statements to summarize your thematic area. You may decide that the original goal statement was adequate, or you may want to revise the statement or combine several statements into a single new statement. Designate a spokesperson for your group.

Your small group's theme(s): ....

....

....

....

....

Revised goal statement(s): ....

....

....

....

....

7. Everyone returns to the **large group**. The designated spokesperson from each small group shares his or her group's goal statements with the large group. The facilitator then records the goal statements and displays them where everyone can see them.

8. As a **large group**, team members discuss any differences of opinions that may have come up over goal selection or wording and attempt to agree on a common set of goals.

9. In the space below, write down the final agreed-upon goal statement(s) for your small group's thematic area. The facilitator should record all of the final goals so they are available for future use.

Final goal statement(s) for your thematic area: ....

....

....

....

....

....

....

➡️ **Proceed to Worksheet 1.3**

After completing either Worksheet 1.1 or 1.2, you are ready to assess your goals based on the six criteria described in this chapter; revise or eliminate any problematic goals; and then set priorities among the remaining ones. Limited resources may prevent you from pursuing all goals simultaneously or with equal effort, or may require you to phase in data collection efforts. Moreover, starting small may be a better strategy for success than tackling all of your goals at once. Delineating clear goal priorities at the outset will help your team organize its improvement efforts.

1. Display or distribute copies of the final goal statements that your team agreed upon when completing Worksheet 1.1 or 1.2. As a **large group**, review the goal statements by discussing the questions listed below. Flag any goal statements that do not meet the following criteria:

· Is the *meaning* of the goals clear? Will the goals yield something of educational value?

. . . .

. . . .

· Can the goals *realistically* be achieved over time?

. . . .

. . . .

· Do the goals *contribute* to an overall vision? Does any goal conflict with the others?

. . . .

. . . .

· Have the goals been *agreed upon* by most team members? By the larger education community? If not, what steps should be taken to obtain broad consensus?

. . . .

. . . .

· Think for a moment about budget, staffing, or political constraints at your site. Should any goals be more or less of a *priority* than others based on these constraints?

. . . .

. . . .

· Can you foresee how you might *measure* progress toward achieving the goals? Will it be possible to establish a performance target for each goal? (It is not necessary to set the actual targets at this time.)

. . . .

. . . .

2. As a **large group**, reexamine any goals that you flagged in Step 1. You may choose either to eliminate or revise a problematic goal. If you decide to revise any of the goals, record the revised goal statements in the space below.

....

....

....

....

....

3. Goals that meet the six criteria described in this chapter should receive higher priority than those that do not. As a **large group**, discuss which goals should receive top priority, beginning with priority number one.

4. Record your final goal statements in priority order below. (It will help you focus your efforts if you have no more than 10 priority goals.)

1. ....

....

2. ....

....

3. ....

....

4. ....

....

5. ....

....

6. ....

....

7. ....

....

8. ....

....

9. ....

....

10. ....

....

Activities 1–5 in this worksheet help you identify specific outcomes and related practices and inputs for the goals you established in Step 1. Complete one worksheet for each goal.

1. Divide your team into small groups of three to five persons, and assign one goal from Worksheet 1.3 to each group. This will make the activity more focused and less time consuming. Depending on the number of people and goals you have, the small groups may need more than one goal to work on.

2. If you have several goals, work on them in order of their priority in Worksheet 1.3. Write down the goal you are currently working on in the space provided.

3. Discuss the specific student outcomes that are implied by your goal, and then record them in the outcomes box.

4. Working backwards, discuss the most important practices and inputs that are related to the specific outcomes you identified and record these in the appropriate boxes. What school practices will help you achieve these student outcomes? What school inputs are likely to influence the practices that are appropriate and the outcomes that are achievable in the short term?

5. Repeat activities 2–4 for each goal you were assigned, using separate worksheets.

Goal

....

....

School Practices	Student Outcomes
Be as specific as possible	*Be as specific as possible*

School Inputs

Be as specific as possible

Worksheet 2.2 helps you evaluate whether the relationships you identified in Worksheet 2.1 are strong enough to justify data collection, support data analysis, and lead to valid conclusions. Complete one worksheet for each goal. Discuss the following questions and note any revisions you would like to make to your set of related outcomes, practices, and inputs.

1. If you have several goals, work on them in order of their priority in Worksheet 1.3. Write down the goal you are currently working on below.

Goal ....

2. Can you be more specific in describing the student outcomes that are implied by your goal?

....

....

....

3. Are you reasonably sure that the school practices you have identified will help you improve or achieve your targeted student outcomes? Which of your identified practices are most strongly linked to your outcomes?

....

....

....

4. How confident are you that the school inputs you have identified influence either the set of practices that are appropriate or the outcomes that are achievable? Which of your identified inputs are most strongly linked to your practices and outcomes?

....

....

....

5. Which of your identified outcomes, practices, and inputs are valued or emphasized the most at your school? Which ones would key stakeholder groups be most interested in knowing something about?

....

....

....

6. Are there any outcomes, practices, or inputs that are receiving attention at your school—because they are recognized either as a problem or as a potential solution—and that should be reflected in your work on this goal?

....

....

....

Worksheet 2.3 helps you narrow your list of related outcomes, practices, and inputs to the most important ones and record them in priority order. Complete one worksheet for each goal.

1. If you have several goals, work on them in order of their priority in Worksheet 1.3. Write down the goal you are currently working on below.

Goal ....

2. Review your notes on Worksheet 2.2. Eliminate or modify any of the outcomes, practices, and inputs you identified in Worksheet 2.1. Record your final selections in priority order below.

Specific student outcomes:

1. ....

2. ....

3. ....

4. ....

5. ....

6. ....

7. ....

8. ....

Related school practices:

1. ....

2. ....

3. ....

4. ....

5. ....

6. ....

7. ....

8. ....

Related school inputs:

1. ....

2. ....

3. ....

4. ....

5. ....

6. ....

7. ....

8. ....

Activities 1–6 in this worksheet help you identify existing and new data sources for the outcomes, practices, and inputs you identified in Worksheet 2.3. You are provided with three copies of the worksheet: "A" for outcomes, "B" for practices, and "C" for inputs. Depending on the number of outcomes, practices, and inputs you identified in Worksheet 2.3, you may need to make additional copies of these worksheets.

1. Write the goal you are working on at the top of the worksheet.

2. Transfer your outcomes from Worksheet 2.3 to the left-hand column of Worksheet 3.1A in order of priority.

3. Discuss with your group or consider on your own where data might be found for each outcome. Write these data sources in the middle column of Worksheet 3.1A. Be expansive. Be

creative. Allow yourself to come up with anything that will provide you with the information you believe will be helpful. You will weed out less important data sources as you continue to develop your indicators.

4. It may be that existing data sources do not provide useful information about the outcomes you have identified. If this is so, space has also been provided in the right-hand column to indicate any crucial new data sources you may need.

5. Repeat activities 1–4 for your practices and inputs, using Worksheets 3.1B and 3.1C, respectively.

6. After completing the worksheet, groups should report the results of their work to the rest of the improvement team.

GOAL:

Outcomes From Worksheet 2.3	Existing Data Sources	Crucial New Data Sources
PRIORITY #_____		
PRIORITY #_____		
PRIORITY #_____		

GOAL:

Practices From Worksheet 2.3	Existing Data Sources	Crucial New Data Sources
PRIORITY # ____		
PRIORITY # ____		
PRIORITY # ____		

GOAL:

Inputs From Worksheet 2.3	Existing Data Sources	Crucial New Data Sources
PRIORITY #_____		
PRIORITY #_____		
PRIORITY #_____		

Activities 1–5 in this worksheet help you develop performance indicators for each data source you identified in Worksheet 3.1. You are provided with three copies of the worksheet: "A" for outcomes, "B" for practices, and "C" for inputs. Depending on the number of outcomes, practices, and inputs you have identified, you may need to make additional copies of these worksheets.

1. Write the goal you are working on at the top of the worksheet.

2. Transfer your outcomes from Worksheet 3.1A to the appropriate boxes in order of priority.

3. For each outcome, think about what you really want to know. Review the different data sources you identified in Worksheet 3.1A. Which data sources will provide you with the most important and relevant information? List the most important ones in order of priority on Worksheet 3.2A.

4. For each data source, think about what information can be produced concerning the associated outcome. Brainstorm with your group or on your own about possible performance indicators that can be derived from the data source and write them in the corresponding boxes. Remember to write your indicators in terms of counts, percents, averages, and rates, and to be as specific as possible. You may identify more than one indicator for each data source.

5. Repeat activities 1–4 for your practices and inputs, using Worksheets 3.2B and 3.2C, respectively.

GOAL:

OUTCOME #_____: ....

Priority Data Sources	Corresponding Performance Indicators
....	....
....	....
....	....
....	....
....	....
....	....

OUTCOME #_____: ....

Priority Data Sources	Corresponding Performance Indicators
....	....
....	....
....	....
....	....
....	....
....	....

OUTCOME #_____: ....

Priority Data Sources	Corresponding Performance Indicators
....	....
....	....
....	....
....	....
....	....
....	....

GOAL:

PRACTICE #_____: ....

Priority Data Sources	Corresponding Performance Indicators

PRACTICE #_____: ....

Priority Data Sources	Corresponding Performance Indicators

PRACTICE #_____: ....

Priority Data Sources	Corresponding Performance Indicators

GOAL:

INPUT #_____: ....

Priority Data Sources	Corresponding Performance Indicators
....	....
....	....
....	....
....	....
....	....
....	....

INPUT #_____: ....

Priority Data Sources	Corresponding Performance Indicators
....	....
....	....
....	....
....	....
....	....
....	....

INPUT #_____: ....

Priority Data Sources	Corresponding Performance Indicators
....	....
....	....
....	....
....	....
....	....
....	....

Activities 1–4 in this worksheet help you refine the performance indicators you identified in Worksheet 3.2. You are provided with three copies of the worksheet: "A" for outcomes, "B" for practices, and "C" for inputs. You may need to make additional copies of these worksheets.

1. Write the goal you are working on at the top of the worksheet.

2. Transfer your outcomes from Worksheet 3.2A to the appropriate boxes in order of priority.

3. For each outcome, review the performance indicators you identified in Worksheet 3.2A and answer the questions listed below. Revise your indicators as needed and record the revised indicators in order of priority in the space provided. You might also find it useful to identify subpopulations whose performance on the indicators you think is important to examine. Repeat this activity for each outcome.

  · Indicators can be expressed as counts, averages, percents, and rates. Each form provides different information. Have you selected the most valuable *numerical forms* for your indicators?

  · Who are your *relevant populations* (the denominators for calculating your indicators)? Should the indicators be rewritten to clarify who the relevant populations are?

  · What *condition(s)* must be met—and when—in order to be counted in each statistic? Should the indicators be rewritten to clarify these conditions?

  · Should you measure *attainment or gains*—or both? Do you need to modify your indicators to do so?

  · What *subpopulations* might you want to compare for each indicator based on demographic characteristics or educational experiences?

4. Repeat activities 1–3 for your practices and inputs, using Worksheets 3.3B and 3.3C, respectively.

GOAL:

OUTCOME #_____: ....

Indicator #1 ....

Indicator #2 ....

Indicator #3 ....

Indicator #4 ....

Indicator #5 ....

Subgroup comparisons ....

....

OUTCOME #_____: ....

Indicator #1 ....

Indicator #2 ....

Indicator #3 ....

Indicator #4 ....

Indicator #5 ....

Subgroup comparisons ....

....

OUTCOME #_____: ....

Indicator #1 ....

Indicator #2 ....

Indicator #3 ....

Indicator #4 ....

Indicator #5 ....

Subgroup comparisons ....

....

GOAL: ....

PRACTICE #_____: ....

Indicator #1 ....

Indicator #2 ....

Indicator #3 ....

Indicator #4 ....

Indicator #5 ....

Subgroup comparisons ....

....

PRACTICE #_____: ....

Indicator #1 ....

Indicator #2 ....

Indicator #3 ....

Indicator #4 ....

Indicator #5 ....

Subgroup comparisons ....

....

PRACTICE #_____: ....

Indicator #1 ....

Indicator #2 ....

Indicator #3 ....

Indicator #4 ....

Indicator #5 ....

Subgroup comparisons ....

....

GOAL:

INPUT #_____: ....

Indicator #1 ....

Indicator #2 ....

Indicator #3 ....

Indicator #4 ....

Indicator #5 ....

Subgroup comparisons ....

....

INPUT #_____: ....

Indicator #1 ....

Indicator #2 ....

Indicator #3 ....

Indicator #4 ....

Indicator #5 ....

Subgroup comparisons ....

....

INPUT #_____: ....

Indicator #1 ....

Indicator #2 ....

Indicator #3 ....

Indicator #4 ....

Indicator #5 ....

Subgroup comparisons ....

....

Activities 1–6 in this worksheet help you assess the quality of your performance indicators and develop a final list of indicators for each outcome, practice, and input. You are provided with three copies of the worksheet: "A" for outcomes, "B" for practices, and "C" for inputs. You may need to make additional copies of these worksheets.

1. Write the goal you are working on at the top of the worksheet.

2. Transfer your outcomes from Worksheet 3.3A to the appropriate boxes in order of priority.

3. For each outcome, review the performance indicators you identified in Worksheet 3.3A and answer the questions listed below. Revise your indicators as needed and record the revised indicators in order of priority in the space provided. Space is also provided to record any thoughts you may have about important subpopulation comparisons, steps to improve accuracy and consistency, actions or decisions to avoid, and steps to guard against distorting the data. Repeat this activity for each outcome.

· How well do the indicators reflect the outcome they are intended to describe? Are there other ways to measure the outcome that provide more valid information?

· What kinds of actions or decisions do you think might be based on the results of these performance indicators? Do you think the quality of the data will support these actions or decisions? What actions or decisions should be avoided so that you do not misuse the data?

· How consistently and accurately are data currently being reported or collected on these indicators? What definitions or data collection practices could be standardized to make the data more reliable?

· Do you think there are any irrelevant factors that might significantly disadvantage or benefit particular groups of students on the indicators? Should any indicators be eliminated or modified in light of this potential bias?

· Are there any indicators that seem particularly susceptible to distortion? What steps might be taken to avoid creating unintended incentives?

4. Repeat activities 1–3 for your practices and inputs, using Worksheets 3.4B and 3.4C, respectively.

5. After completing the worksheet, groups should report the results of their work to the rest of the improvement team.

6. Give one copy of the completed worksheet to your meeting facilitator for the project files.

GOAL:

OUTCOME #_____: . . . .

Indicator #1 . . . .

Indicator #2 . . . .

Indicator #3 . . . .

Indicator #4 . . . .

Indicator #5 . . . .

Notes . . . .

. . . .

OUTCOME #_____: . . . .

Indicator #1 . . . .

Indicator #2 . . . .

Indicator #3 . . . .

Indicator #4 . . . .

Indicator #5 . . . .

Notes . . . .

. . . .

OUTCOME #_____: . . . .

Indicator #1 . . . .

Indicator #2 . . . .

Indicator #3 . . . .

Indicator #4 . . . .

Indicator #5 . . . .

Notes . . . .

. . . .

GOAL:

PRACTICE #_____: ....

Indicator #1 ....

Indicator #2 ....

Indicator #3 ....

Indicator #4 ....

Indicator #5 ....

Notes ....

....

PRACTICE #_____: ....

Indicator #1 ....

Indicator #2 ....

Indicator #3 ....

Indicator #4 ....

Indicator #5 ....

Notes ....

....

PRACTICE #_____: ....

Indicator #1 ....

Indicator #2 ....

Indicator #3 ....

Indicator #4 ....

Indicator #5 ....

Notes ....

....

GOAL:

INPUT #_____ : ....

Indicator #1 ....

Indicator #2 ....

Indicator #3 ....

Indicator #4 ....

Indicator #5 ....

Notes ....

....

INPUT #_____ : ....

Indicator #1 ....

Indicator #2 ....

Indicator #3 ....

Indicator #4 ....

Indicator #5 ....

Notes ....

....

INPUT #_____ : ....

Indicator #1 ....

Indicator #2 ....

Indicator #3 ....

Indicator #4 ....

Indicator #5 ....

Notes ....

....

Activities 1–8 in this worksheet help you develop a plan for collecting data on your final list of performance indicators. You are provided with three copies of the worksheet: "A" for outcomes, "B" for practices, and "C" for inputs. You may need to make additional copies of these worksheets.

1. Write the goal you are working on at the top of the worksheet.

2. Transfer your outcome indicators from Worksheet 3.4A to the first column of Worksheet 3.5A.

3. Refer back to Worksheet 3.2A to determine the data sources for your indicators. Not all of your indicators may be reflected on Worksheet 3.2A, since you may have added indicators in subsequent steps. For new indicators, think about where you will obtain the relevant data. Record all data sources and locations for your final indicators in the second column of Worksheet 3.5A.

4. Discuss and record what next steps need to be taken to obtain the indicator data.

5. Discuss and record who will assume primary responsibility for the next steps.

6. Decide on a target date for each next step.

7. Repeat steps 1–6 for your practice and input indicators, using Worksheets 3.5B and 3.5C, respectively.

8. Give one copy of the completed worksheet to your meeting facilitator for the project files.

WORKSHEET 3.5A • Developing a Data Collection Plan for Outcome Indicators

GOAL:

Outcome Indicators from Worksheet 3.4A	Data Source/Location from Worksheet 3.2A	Next Steps	Person Responsible	Target Date

At Your Fingertips: Using Everyday Data to Improve Schools © 1998 MPR Associates, Inc.

GOAL:

Practice Indicators from Worksheet 3.4B	Data Source/Location from Worksheet 3.2B	Next Steps	Person Responsible	Target Date

GOAL:

Input Indicators from Worksheet 3.4C	Data Source/Location from Worksheet 3.2C	Next Steps	Person Responsible	Target Date

Copy the goal, outcome, and indicator you are currently working on from Worksheet 3.4A, and then discuss the questions under 1–5 below and record your responses in the spaces provided.

Goal ....

Outcome #_____: ....

Indicator #_____: ....

1. Getting to Know Your Data

What is the data source for this indicator? ....

What is the unit of measurement? ....

Who or what is included in the statistic? ....

What is the size of the denominator (if applicable)? ....

What is the time period covered? ....

What additional information do you need to understand the data you are working with? ....

....

2. Your First Impressions

Does your performance on the indicator in question seem high? Low? Does it match your expectations? How? ....

....

....

Translate the data into concrete terms (the number of persons, days, classes, courses, and so on, that are affected): ....

....

Does this information contribute anything to your understanding of the data? If so, what? ....

....

....

3. Examining the Spread, or Distribution, of Your Data

You may want to graph or otherwise examine the distribution of your data.

What is the average (mean) of the data? ....

What do you think should be an acceptable average (mean)? Why? ....

....

3. Examining the Spread, or Distribution, of Your Data—continued

What is the range of your data? Highest value _____ Lowest value _____

What do you think should be an acceptable range? Why? ....

....

Are there any outliers (extreme high or low values that are distorting the mean)? If so, what are they?

....

Do you think your outlying performers have particular needs that should be addressed? If so, what might they be?

....

Divide your data either into *quartiles* (highest 25 percent, upper middle 25 percent, lower middle 25 percent, lowest 25 percent) or *deciles* (10 equal parts).

Which groups, if any, exhibit exemplary performance? Satisfactory performance? Unsatisfactory performance?

....

4. Subgroup Comparisons

Referring back to Worksheets 3.3A and 3.4A, what subgroup comparisons did you conclude were important to make on this indicator (based on different student demographics or educational experiences)?

....

Are any student groups performing better or worse than the others? If so, what patterns emerge? ....

....

What is the magnitude of these differences or trends? Are they practically important? ....

....

If the data are based on a random sample rather than an entire population, are the perceived differences statistically significant?

....

5. Interpreting Your Data

How do you think your school is performing on the indicator in question? ....

....

....

What do the distribution of your data and your subgroup comparisons suggest about how improvement efforts should be focused?

....

....

What additional information do you need to understand or interpret these data? ....

....

Copy the goal, practice, and indicator you are currently working on from Worksheet 3.4B, and then discuss the questions under 1–5 below and record your responses in the spaces provided.

Goal ....

Practice #_____: ....

Indicator #_____: ....

1. Getting to Know Your Data

What is the data source for this indicator? ....

What is the unit of measurement? ....

Who or what is included in the statistic? ....

What is the size of the denominator (if applicable)? ....

What is the time period covered? ....

What additional information do you need to understand the data you are working with? ....

....

2. Your First Impressions

Does your performance on the indicator in question seem high? Low? Does it match your expectations? How?

....

....

Translate the data into concrete terms (the number of persons, days, classes, courses, and so on, that are affected):

....

Does this information contribute anything to your understanding of the data? If so, what? ....

....

....

3. Examining the Spread, or Distribution, of Your Data

You may want to graph or otherwise examine the distribution of your data.

What is the average (mean) of the data? ....

What do you think should be an acceptable average (mean)? Why? ....

....

3. Examining the Spread, or Distribution, of Your Data—continued

What is the range of your data? Highest value _____ Lowest value _____

What do you think should be an acceptable range? Why? . . . .

. . . .

Are there any outliers (extreme high or low values that are distorting the mean)? If so, what are they?

. . . .

Do you think your outlying performers have particular needs that should be addressed? If so, what might they be?

. . . .

Divide your data either into *quartiles* (highest 25 percent, upper middle 25 percent, lower middle 25 percent, lowest 25 percent) or *deciles* (10 equal parts).

Which groups, if any, exhibit exemplary performance? Satisfactory performance? Unsatisfactory performance?

. . . .

4. Subgroup Comparisons

Referring back to Worksheets 3.3B and 3.4B, what subgroup comparisons did you conclude were important to make on this indicator (based on different teacher or classroom characteristics, for example)? . . . .

. . . .

Are any practices more (or less) prevalent in particular circumstances than others? If so, what patterns emerge?

. . . .

What is the magnitude of these differences or trends? Are they practically important? . . . .

. . . .

If the data are based on a random sample rather than an entire population, are the perceived differences statistically significant?

. . . .

5. Interpreting Your Data

How do you think your school is performing on the indicator in question? . . . .

. . . .

. . . .

How do these practice data contribute to your understanding of your related outcome data? . . . .

. . . .

. . . .

What additional information do you need to understand or interpret these data? . . . .

. . . .

Copy the goal, input, and indicator you are currently working on from Worksheet 3.4C, and then discuss the questions under 1–5 below and record your responses in the spaces provided.

Goal ....

Input #_____: ....

Indicator #_____: ....

1. Getting to Know Your Data

What is the data source for this indicator? ....

What is the unit of measurement? ....

Who or what is included in the statistic? ....

What is the size of the denominator (if applicable)? ....

What is the time period covered? ....

What additional information do you need to understand the data you are working with? ....

....

2. Your First Impressions

Does your performance on the indicator in question seem high? Low? Does it match your expectations? How?

....

....

Translate the data into concrete terms (the number of persons, days, classes, courses, and so on, that are affected):

....

Does this information contribute anything to your understanding of the data? If so, what? ....

....

....

3. Examining the Spread, or Distribution, of Your Data

You may want to graph or otherwise examine the distribution of your data.

What is the average (mean) of the data? ....

If applicable, what do you think should be an acceptable average (mean)? Why? ....

....

3. Examining the Spread, or Distribution, of Your Data—continued

What is the range of your data? Highest value _____ Lowest value _____

If applicable, what do you think should be an acceptable range? Why? ....

Are there any outliers (extreme high or low values that are distorting the mean)? If so, what are they? ....

....

Do you think the outlying data require particular attention? If so, what might this be? ....

....

Divide your data either into *quartiles* (highest 25 percent, upper middle 25 percent, lower middle 25 percent, lowest 25 percent) or *deciles* (10 equal parts).

How widely dispersed are the data? Does this raise any concerns? If so, what are they? ....

....

4. Subgroup Comparisons

Referring back to Worksheets 3.3C and 3.4C, what subgroup comparisons did you conclude were important to make on this indicator (based on different buildings, departments, or programs in your school, for example)?

....

Are there important differences in inputs in different circumstances? If so, what patterns emerge? ....

....

What is the magnitude of these differences or trends? Are they practically important? ....

....

If the data are based on a random sample rather than an entire population, are the perceived differences statistically significant?

....

5. Interpreting Your Data

How do you think your school is performing on the indicator in question? ....

....

....

How do these input data contribute to your understanding of your related outcome data? ....

....

....

What additional information do you need to understand or interpret these data? ....

....

Write down the goal you are working on below. After examining all of your indicator data on the outcomes, practices, and inputs related to this goal, it is time to summarize your findings. Review all copies of Worksheets 4.1A–4.1C for this goal, and then discuss the questions under 1–4 below. Record your responses in the spaces provided.

Goal ....

1. Deciding on the Implications of Your Indicator Data

How do you think your school is performing on this goal? ....

....

....

What evidence do you have to support this opinion? ....

....

Why do you think you are performing at the current level? Cite specific evidence, where possible.

....

....

What additional information do you need to understand your performance on this goal? ....

....

2. Examining Relationships Among Your Outcome, Practice, and Input Data

Refer back to Worksheet 2.3 to review the outcomes, practices, and inputs you decided were related to this goal.

Are there any relationships between pairs of specific outcomes, practices, and inputs that might help you better understand your performance on this goal? If so, what are they? ....

....

....

Graph or examine the relationship between the relevant indicators for key pairs of outcomes, practices, and inputs. Do the data appear to move in the same direction, in opposite directions, or do they appear to be unaffected by one another?

....

....

How does examining these relationships contribute to your understanding of your performance on this goal? Remember, correlation does not imply causation. ....

....

....

3. Presenting Your Findings

To prepare for presenting your findings to the entire improvement team (or additional audiences), decide what are the most important points you would like to make about how your school is performing on this education goal. . . . .

. . . .

. . . .

. . . .

. . . .

How would you illustrate each of these points? Your choices include single statistics, tables, and graphs (frequency distributions, pie charts, bar graphs, line graphs, and scatterplots).

. . . .

. . . .

. . . .

. . . .

Who will be responsible for:

· Preparing the presentation materials . . . .

· Making the presentation . . . .

· Additional research . . . .

4. Improving Your Indicator Data

What performance indicators related to this goal would you eliminate in the future? . . . .

. . . .

. . . .

What performance indicators would you add to help better understand your performance on this goal? . . . .

. . . .

. . . .

What existing data sources need to be improved? How? . . . .

. . . .

. . . .

What new data sources need to be developed? . . . .

. . . .

. . . .

Goal ....

1. Review all of your copies of Worksheet 4.1A for the above goal, then copy your outcome indicators and the current level of performance on them below. Do not fill in your targets yet.

Outcome Indicators	Current Performance	Your Target
....	....	....
....	....	....
....	....	....
....	....	....

2. After gathering information about desirable levels of performance on the above outcome indicators, summarize below what you learned from

State and national performance standards: ....

....

....

....

Input from important stakeholder groups: ....

....

....

....

Exemplary school or program performance: ....

....

....

....

State or national averages: ....

....

....

....

At Your Fingertips: Using Everyday Data to Improve Schools © 1998 MPR Associates, Inc.

3. Based on your research, answer the following questions, and then fill in your proposed performance targets for each outcome indicator:

What specific performance targets did you identify in your search? . . . .

. . . .

. . . .

. . . .

. . . .

Based on the information you gathered, how satisfied are you with your current performance on the above indicators?

. . . .

. . . .

. . . .

. . . .

If you discovered several different performance targets, what do you believe is the most appropriate target given your circumstances? . . . .

. . . .

. . . .

. . . .

4. After proposing performance targets, discuss the following and revise your targets as necessary:

Is the target realistic and does it incorporate high expectations? . . . .

. . . .

. . . .

What does the target mean in practical terms? Is this reasonable? . . . .

. . . .

. . . .

What time frame is realistic for attaining the targets? . . . .

. . . .

. . . .

. . . .

Goal . . . .

1. Review the performance targets you proposed in Worksheet 5.1 as well as Worksheets 4.1B and C for the above goal, and then discuss the following with your team:

How satisfied are you that your current practices and improvement strategies will help you attain the performance targets listed on Worksheet 5.1? . . . .

. . . .

. . . .

What performance targets, if any, are not being addressed by current practices and improvement strategies?

. . . .

. . . .

What changes do you think need to occur in current inputs, practices, and improvement strategies in order to attain the targets? . . . .

. . . .

. . . .

. . . .

2. Consider the following questions to help plan an appropriate course of action:

What evidence exists to support the improvement strategies you are considering (for example, from exemplary schools and programs, national professional organizations, school reform networks, state and national education agencies, and the educational research literature)? . . . .

. . . .

. . . .

How confident are you that the proposed changes in inputs, practices, and improvement strategies will lead to improved performance on your indicators? . . . .

. . . .

. . . .

Are the proposed changes consistent with your overall goals?

. . . .

. . . .

. . . .

For each goal, list your outcome, practice, and input indicators and corresponding baseline data, performance targets, and projected time frames. Then summarize your related improvement strategies in the space provided.

GOAL:

Priority Indicators	Baseline	Target	Time Frame
Outcome Indicators			
Practice Indicators			

Priority Indicators	Baseline	Target	Time Frame
Input Indicators			

Summary of improvement strategies for this goal:

This worksheet helps you review the development of your indicators, decide on a final list of priority indicators for ongoing data collection purposes, plan the timing of your data collection and analysis, and decide where the data will be stored.

1. Write down the education goal you are working on below.

2. Review the following worksheets related to this goal: 2.3—Finalizing Your Related Outcomes, Practices, and Inputs; 3.4—Developing a Final List of Outcome, Practice, and Input Indicators; and 4.2—Summarizing Your Findings, especially Part 4 on improving your indicator data. Decide which indicators are most important for understanding your progress toward achieving your goal, and list them in priority order in the appropriate outcome,

practice, or input section below or on the next page. Be realistic about how much data you can collect and review on an ongoing basis, and list only the most important indicators.

3. Think about the timing of data collection and analysis for each of your indicators, and note your suggestions below. Consider when the data usually become available; how the timing of data collection could influence data quality; how frequently the data should be reviewed to support ongoing adjustments in practices or long-term planning; when important local decisions are made; and the time frames you set in Worksheet 5.3 for achieving your performance targets.

4. Decide where the data should be stored to facilitate updating and analyzing these data and to respect confidentiality concerns.

GOAL:

Priority Outcome Indicators	Timing of Data Collection/Analysis	Data Storage Location
1.		
2.		
3.		
4.		
5.		
6.		
7.		
8.		
9.		
10.		

Priority Practice Indicators	Timing of Data Collection/Analysis	Data Storage Location
1.		
2.		
3.		
4.		
5.		
6.		
7.		
8.		
9.		
10.		

Priority Input Indicators	Timing of Data Collection/Analysis	Data Storage Location
1.		
2.		
3.		
4.		
5.		
6.		
7.		
8.		
9.		
10.		

This worksheet helps you identify indicators, data sources, and data stores that need improving or developing, and devise a plan for building your capacity in these areas.

1. Write down the education goal you are working on below.

2. Review Worksheet 4.2—Summarizing Your Findings, which is related to this goal. Especially review Part 4 on improving your indicator data. Identify any existing indicators or data sources that need to be improved, and list these in the first column of Part A. Decide what needs to be done (such as standardizing key definitions or data collection and reporting practices to make the data more reliable; who will be responsible; and what your target date is for completing this work.

3. Review all copies of Worksheet 3.1—Identifying Data Sources, which is related to this goal. In combination with Part 4 of Worksheet 4.2, identify any crucial new data sources or indicators that need to be developed, and list these in the first column of Part B. Decide what needs to be done (such as forming a committee to develop the source, researching appropriate data collection and scoring methods, and developing survey or test items); who will be responsible; and what your target date is for completing this work.

4. Review the rest of Worksheet 4.2 and decide what types of analyses you want to perform that are related to this goal. In particular, consider whether you need to keep records for individual students (or teachers or others) or maintain longitudinal data (that is, two or more data points for the same students or others obtained at different points in time). Decide what stores of data need to be modified or developed, and list these in the first column of Part C. Describe what needs to be done (such as developing an automated individual record system or adding data elements to an existing one); who will be responsible; and what your target date is for completing this work.

GOAL:

A. Existing Indicators or Data Sources Needing Improvement	What Needs to Be Done?	Person(s) Responsible	Target Date
1.			
2.			
3.			
4.			

Worksheet 6.2 continued

B. New Indicators or Data Sources Needing Development	What Needs to Be Done?	Person(s) Responsible	Target Date
1.	....	....	....
2.	....	....	....
3.	....	....	....
4.	....	....	....

C. Data Stores Needing Improvement or Development	What Needs to Be Done?	Person(s) Responsible	Target Date
1.	....	....	....
2.	....	....	....
3.	....	....	....
4.	....	....	....

This worksheet helps you identify and interpret trends in your performance.

1. Write down the goal you are working on in the space provided on the following sample report card.

2. Copy your priority performance indicators related to this goal from Worksheet 6.1 and place them in the left-hand column of the report card.

3. Copy your performance targets from Worksheet 5.3 and place them in the right-hand column of the report card. (If you have added indicators in Step 6, you may need to set performance targets for them using Worksheet 5.1.)

4. Fill in your baseline data and any trend data you have collected up to now. Add successive data points as they become available. Space is provided for five years of performance data. In order to interpret your entire performance on a goal, you should analyze all of your related indicators at the same time. The assumption made here is that you review your entire performance on a goal annually, although you may choose to do so using a different time interval (such as once a semester or once every two years). In addition to this effort, you may also choose to review your performance on individual indicators at various times, as recorded in Worksheet 6.1.

5. Beginning with your outcome data, you may want to graph any important or interesting indicators.

6. For each outcome indicator, note the direction and consistency of the trend. Is there a general or consistent trend in the data? Is the trend positive, negative, or holding steady? Is there a break in the data, indicating that a trend is changing its direction?

· ·

7. For each outcome indicator, how confident are you that a trend exists? How many data points do you have to date? How large are the year-to-year changes? To what extent might these changes be due to measurement error? What might be sources of inaccuracy in collecting or reporting these data?

· ·

8. If you are confident that a trend exists in your outcome data, what do you think might help explain this trend? What changes in key inputs or practices or what specific improvement strategies do you think may be responsible for it? What evidence is there among your practice and input indicator data to support your hypotheses?

....

....

....

....

....

....

9. Are your outcomes moving in different directions? What might explain this?

....

....

....

....

10. Do you have enough information to understand the trends in your data? What additional information do you need?

....

....

....

....

11. You may want to investigate whether your school has implemented key improvement strategies in the way that was intended. Have teachers changed their instructional practices? Do all teachers define the improvement strategies in the same way? Is the school supporting implementation of the improvement strategies in the manner initially planned?

....

....

....

....

12. Is there strong evidence to support changing your current course of action? If so, what do you think needs to be done?

....

....

....

....

Sample Report Card						
GOAL:						
Performance Indicators	**Year** ___	**Year** ___	**Year** ___	**Year** ___	**Year** ___	**Target**
Outcome Indicators:						
Related Practice Indicators:						
Related Input Indicators:						

This worksheet helps you develop an organized communication strategy.

1. Decide who your audience(s) should be. Who would be interested in your general performance or in your performance on a specific goal or indicator? Who might be affected by your findings? Consider stakeholders both inside and outside your school. You may identify multiple audiences with different interests.

. . . .

. . . .

. . . .

2. Decide what your purpose is in communicating your progress to each of your audiences. What do you hope to get out of this effort?

. . . .

. . . .

. . . .

3. Decide what the appropriate forum is for communicating your progress to each audience (for instance, an informal meeting, panel discussion, formal presentation, school report card, newsletter, or school improvement report). Decide if it is best to communicate your findings in a written format, verbally, or both.

. . . .

. . . .

. . . .

. . . .

4. Decide when and how often you should communicate your progress to your different audiences.

. . . .

. . . .

. . . .

5. Decide what the content of your presentation or product should be. What do your audiences want and need to know? What background or supporting information will help your audiences understand the data?

. . . .

. . . .

. . . .

. . . .

This worksheet helps you revise your performance indicator system so that it continues to produce useful information over time and supports continuous improvement at your school. Periodically, you should consider the following questions and determine whether you need to revisit any of the six steps in this workbook.

	Yes/Maybe	No/Unlikely
· Have your school's education goals changed?	☐	☐
If yes or maybe, return to Step 1 and work forward.		
· Have your improvement strategies changed?	☐	☐
If yes or maybe, return to Step 2 and work forward.		
· Have any new data sources become available or old ones become obsolete?	☐	☐
If yes or maybe, return to Step 3 and work forward.		
· Should you eliminate, add, or reformulate any performance indicators to make them more reliable or relevant?	☐	☐
If yes or maybe, return to Step 3 and work forward.		
· Should you reset any performance targets, either because they have already been met or are unrealistic?	☐	☐
If yes or maybe, return to Step 5 and work forward.		
· Do you need to modify your improvement strategies, either because some have proven to be ineffective or counterproductive or because evidence suggests a new approach is called for?	☐	☐
If yes or maybe, return to Step 5 and work forward.		
· Do you need to modify your data collection and storage procedures?	☐	☐
If yes or maybe, return to Step 6.		
· Has the schedule for collecting and examining your data and communicating your findings been working well or should you modify it?	☐	☐
If yes or maybe, return to Step 6.		
· Has communication with your different stakeholder groups been effective or do you need to revise your communication strategy?	☐	☐
If yes or maybe, return to Step 6.		
· Have you identified any other problems related to implementation or use of your performance indicator system?	☐	☐
If yes or maybe, return to Step 6.		